Deadlines, Headlines & Porcupines:
The Laugh Lines Behind the Bylines

With miles of smiles!

☺ Ann Hauprich

UNITED STATES CATALOGUING
IN PUBLICATION DATA

Hauprich, Ann
Deadlines Headlines & Porcupines:
The Laugh Lines Behind the Bylines

Illustrations by Steve Nease

ISBN 9780971462045

Library of Congress Control Number
2006905230

Published by PECKHAVEN PUBLISHING
178 Wagman's Ridge Road, Saratoga Springs, NY 12866
www.joepeckonline.com

Printed by IBT GLOBAL
18 Industrial Park Road, Troy, NY 12180
www.integratedbook.com

Typesetting & pagination by
ANN HAUPRICH COMMUNICATIONS
PO Box 2782, Malta, NY 12020
www.annhauprich.com

Dedicated to my FUNderful parents,
Audrey & Donald Hauprich,
who built a home for their
10 children on a firm foundation
of faith, hope, love & laughter
and to my three daughters,
Tara, Marietje & Kiersten,
who humored me each time I cried:
"Someday we'll look back
on this and laugh."

Table of Contents

PROLOGUE
The story behind the cover story
Steve Nease: A cartoonist with character................................8
Which came first: The chicken on
my shoulder or the egg on my face?..............................13
Deep laugh lines have deep roots....................................17

NOTHING TO CROW ABOUT
Notes on being a freelance writer & other
funny business along the publishing path
Cooped up author hatches plot to nab Pullet Surprise............24
So ... this is why writers stopped using quill pens!.................26
Where there's smoke . . . there's a wood stove.....................28
City cook in a country kitchen: recipe for disaster.................32
Etiquette for entertaining stranded country couriers............35
The truth about false labor; the stork went on strike...........36
Schooling at Mother's Knee: Lessons in life from A - Z.........42

THE PLOT THICKENS
(With apologies to Dickens)
Why I went to the woods only to flee the forest 48
Dipping, slipping & sliding into life on a lake 50

A SERIOUS LOOK AT LAUGHING MATTERS
Dr. Goodman's prescription for fractured funny bones..........54
Ms. Ingram enjoys helping others humor their stress............57

HUMOR: DON'T LEAVE HOME WITHOUT IT!
The overseas holiday that almost went up in flames..............62
A near death (by mortification) experience 64
You can't win a spraying match with a skunk........................66

EXTRA! EXTRA! READ ALL ABOUT
. . . SOME EXTRA PLAYFUL SOULS
It's easy to kid around with these grown-ups

Bear hunting . . . the Agnes Pompa way 70
Mike Fitzgerald's sweet Saratoga success story.......................72
Zucchinis serve fun & healthy entertainment 74
British actor steals show on American battlefield 76
History on tap at bubbly curator's bottle museum.................79
Bob Kovachick: Sunny with a chance of laughter......................82
Map company founder needed little direction.........................84
Why baker Patty Rutland really takes the cake 87
Michael Noonan's picture perfect dog, Tudd...........................90
Ed & Maureen Lewi: A match made in PR heaven.....................92
Joseph Bruchac III: Rambo in moccasins?................................96

WHO SAID "NEVER THE TWAIN SHALL MEET"?
Mark my words, Rudyard! 'Tis not always so!

David Hyde Pierce: Always a class act 102
More than just a few minutes with Andy Rooney....................112
Why there's so much ado about Marylou.............................120
Mary Ann Mobley: From 90210 to 12020 126
Maestro Dutoit and "The Magic Baton"...............................132

LAUGH TILL THE COWS COME HOME
Meet the folks at Peckhaven Publishing....................................136

EGG-STRA SPECIAL ACKNOWLEDGMENTS
I couldn't have done it without you 140

SKAAL! A LITERARY TOAST TO ROTARY
Why a portion of the proceeds from the sale of this book
will be donated to Rotary-sponsored literary programs........142

COMING IN 2007
Ballston Spa: The Way We Were; The Way We Are............146

NEED A FEW MORE LAUGH LINES?
This order form makes it easy to share with others.............148

PROLOGUE

The story behind the cover story

Steve Nease
A cartoonist with character

Exactly a quarter of a century ago, a budding editorial cartoonist working at a community newspaper on the outskirts of Toronto sketched a swanky, lanky cigar-puffing stork to be used as a decoration at the baby shower for one of his co-workers. Although the poster board on which the stork was conceived using black ink accented with pink and blue highlighters is now a shade of mellow yellow, the image will be given a place of honor at the 25th birthday party for my firstborn child later this year. And, barring a burglary, the masterpiece will be the centerpiece when the first of my grandchildren arrives -- hopefully less than 25 years from now!

The reason the stork is cherished in a manner that is normally reserved for a priceless family heirloom is that it IS a priceless family heirloom . . . an original, one-of-a-kind signed work by a gifted artist who has since earned the admiration and respect of legions of fans from Atlantic to Pacific. A six-time recipient of the Canadian Community Newspapers Awards for editorial cartooning, Steve's creations hang on the walls of personalities ranging from former Hockey Night in Canada broadcaster Don Cherry to high-ranking Members of Parliament. This, however, is not the reason the stork is priceless to me. It is a treasure beyond measure because it was a gift from the heart of a cartoonist of truly remarkable character.

From the time I first met Steve in the late 1970s at The Oakville Journal Record (which later amalgamated with The Oakville Beaver), I was impressed with his ability to combine a sense of humor with a sense of integrity. His insightfulness -- the uncanny ability to read between the lines and cut to the chase under intense deadline pressure -- never ceased to amaze me and other staff members.

Whether the issue involved a raging political firestorm or a smoldering social justice issue -- like responsibility for keeping the homeless warm -- Steve wasted no time sharpening his pencil and producing a picture that sharpened our perspective.

But it was in 1984 that the mostly self-taught artist who insists he got into cartooning by sheer accident began producing cartoons that REALLY hit home when he introduced a family comic strip called PUD. Originally limited to a small local audience, the Pud strips now brighten the lives of legions from coast-to-coast via Canadian Artists Syndicate – the same corporation that syndicates his editorial cartoons.

"The strip is based on my own family -- with only the slightest poetic license," quips Steve, noting he literally draws inspiration from his wife, Dian, and their four children: Robert, Ben, Sammy and Max. "One day it just occurred to me that I had not only a steady stream of ideas, but also a natural cast of characters to go with them," he muses. At the time the first comic strip was published in The Oakville Beaver, Steve and Dian were adjusting to the birth of their second son, Ben, whom they had affectionately dubbed Pud. It is a testament to Steve's creative genius that, 22 years later, the strip is more popular than ever. The fact that Ben and his older brother, Robert, are now in their twenties has not diminished Pud's appeal. Faithful readers follow the strip like a long-running sit-com.

"As Ben and Robert got older and Sammy and Max (now 16 and 9) joined our family; the strip just sort of evolved," he reflects. "I remember situations rather than just snapshots so for me the strip provides a vivid reminder of what our family life's really been like. . . . Pud is a kind of an animated family album -- with no posed shots."

Creating Pud is but one of the many deadlines Steve must meet as art director of The Oakville Beaver and as a thought-provoking editorial cartoonist. In addition to having his cartoons grace the pages of more than 70 newspapers, hundreds of others have been featured in a broad spectrum of books and periodicals on both sides of the border, including *Chicken Soup for the Parent's Soul* and such titillating titles as *Father Knows Zilch: A Guide for Dumbfounded Dads* by hard-wired for satire Canadian columnist Linwood Barclay – with whom both Steve and I had the pleasure of working during his Oakville Journal Record days.

Ever humble, Steve says the "biggest thrill" and "highest compliment" he can think of is when he enters a home or office where's he's never been before and spots one of his Pud comic strips that's yellowed with age held to a refrigerator or a filing cabinet with a magnet.

This was tried with the stork poster once, but its magnetic personality was so strong that it was drawn to higher ground -- it prefers to hang on a wall inside of a frame!

Knowing that Steve prefers sap to run down maple trees for use as syrup rather than sticking pages containing his artwork together, I now invite you to read "the story behind the story" of the cover illustration by Steve Nease that inspired the opening chapters of this literary labor of love and laughter. By the way, if any one asks where this book came from, tell them the stork brought it, eh?!

It is my great honor and privilege to reprint a sampling of some of Steve's Pud cartoons along with a reproduction of the stork he made for my 1981 baby shower and a caricature he did for my parents' 35th wedding anniversary -- they just celebrated their 58th, but I'll let you do the math!

Last, but far from least, I am tickled to share a classy pen and ink drawing he presented to me when I resigned as News Editor of The Oakville Beaver in 1983 in the hope of being able to spend more quality time with then only child: Tara. (In a nifty twist, Tara helped to design the pages inside this book that showcase Steve's artwork!)

Looking perky and preppy despite having a toddler tugging on the hem of my skirt along with a stack of newspapers and an Underwood Five typewriter on either side of a marquee for ANNIE, the farewell gift bears the inscription:

"To a very special lady, with my deepest respect. NEASE, 15-7-83.

Is it any wonder, tears of joy fill my eyes as I type this tribute:

To a very special gent, with my deepest respect -- topped with mounds of gratitude for your incredibly positive attitude. ANNIE. 15-6-06.

What came first:
The chicken on my shoulder
or the egg on my face?

Long before Steve Nease drew the caricature of me that adorns the cover of this book, I often felt like a comic book character just waiting to come to life. While not exactly the glamorous Brenda Starr reporter type, I wasn't quite as pathetic as Orphan Annie either. Leave it to Steve to create the perfect hybrid: Little Annie Looney!

Sketched in a fictitious setting some place between Broadway and the broad side of a barn, the scene crafted by the artist prompted me to ponder that age old question: What came first: The chicken on my shoulder or the egg on my face?

If you don't see the egg, it's because you missed the first draft of *Deadlines, Headlines & Porcupines: The Laugh Lines Behind the Bylines* when it made what might charitably be called its laughable literary debut just before the turn-of-the-millennium.

Consisting of about 48 pages, the literally spineless wanna-be-book had the look of something that had been copied, collated and stapled at a local quick print franchise because -- funnily enough -- that's exactly what happened. The bulk of the copies of the forerunner to the volume you now hold in your hands were mostly given away as stocking stuffers to family and friends who were then nervously awaiting the arrival of the year 2000. To be or not to be OK on Y2K? That was the question of the day!

My sole consolation as I look back is that I provided people who were hoarding flashlights and jugs of water something to laugh about. But in the end, the joke was on me. In the era of the UN-Cola, I became the author of the UN-book. Although not visible to the naked (or even semi-clad) eye, there was egg on my face as well as a chicken on my shoulder when the rooster crowed as the sun rose on January 1, 2000.

If you happen to be one of the few people outside of my circle of family who owns one of the originals, please feel free to contact me about trading it in for the real deal. I, in turn, will put your relic in a makeshift museum of items from 1999 that have the distinction of being as scarce as hen's teeth! Time and again I dreamed of adding more chapters to the original collection of 10 essays.

Time and again the demands of motherhood combined with those of establishing a periodical called *Saratoga Living* (originally subtitled *"The magazine that showcases the faces behind the places"*) on top of editing a monthly newspaper that was then published by The Anastos Media Group, made it impossible for me to squeeze in any creative writing on the side.

Complications from a hysterical-ectomy followed by a parting of the matrimonial waters made things all the more challenging at the start of 2001, but the unsinkable PollyANNIE in me soon established a new home office -- this time within hiking or biking distance of just about everything in the charming upstate New York village of Ballston Spa where I had spent some of the most joyous days of my youth.

The days flew by as I juggled single parenting with being an editor, publisher, advertising director, circulation manager, page designer, paginator and overall chief cook and bottle washer. Suffice to say I crashed more than once while reading bedtime stories to my youngest!

14

Alas! I learned the hard way that computers also crash. The worst episode resulted in the loss of a decade's worth of my *Words of Art*. Everything I had written during the better part of the 1990s was deemed forever "Lost In (Cyber) Space" when the hard drive of my PC fried like an egg one dark and stormy night.   All the king's horses and all the king's computer repairmen couldn't put my portfolio back together again.

Then came 9/11 followed a year later by the lengthy hospitalization and even lengthier convalescence of my normally on-the-go eldest. After trying to do the impossible well for another year and a half, I finally made the toughest decision of my life: that of selling the magazine that was so near and dear to my heart to a company that was blessed with the resources needed to make it blossom into the vibrant periodical it is today.

Although the new owners graciously kept me on as editor during the transitional period, I ultimately came to the realization that I was at my happiest when I was writing stories that touched hearts, lifted spirits and tickled funny bones. Changing my job title from editor to writer in January of 2005 enabled me to provide for my young uns as well as two sled dogs (adopted shortly after the passing of our beloved Max), two purr-fectly frisky cats and two cagey guinea pigs without needing to work the 80-plus hours a week I'd been averaging since launching the periodical in 1998.

The funny thing was, I couldn't seem to write anything of a humorous nature. The who, what, why, where, when and how stuff still flowed, but as silly as it may sound, it felt as if my funny bone was broken. After dusting off an interview I had conducted with HUMOResilience specialist Margie Ingram, I determined to bounce back -- even if I landed on my sassafras a few times before taking flight as a writer.

Accepting an invitation from Margie and her husband, Dr. Joel Goodman, founder and director of The HUMOR Project, to attend the 20th annual Humor Conference at which Yakov Smirnoff and Teri Garr were keynote speakers in April of 2005 proved to be another turning point.

There are no words to adequately thank Joel, Margie and their band of merry men and women for the miles of smiles and infusion of infectious laughter that came my way as I attended sessions with such titles as "Why is Everyone So Cranky? Life Isn't A Duress Rehearsal" and "HA!! HA! Healthy Aging! Humorous Aging!"

One of my assignments in the latter class was to create a rhyme or other verse that could be performed to the tune of a favorite melody . . . such as "Twinkle, Twinkle Little Star."

I now invite you and your favorite sidekick to get out a harmonica so one of you can provide the instrumentals while the other one belts out the following lyrics to the tune of that popular childhood song.

Wrinkle, wrinkle, little lines
Creep along my face like vines
Making people think I'm old
When I still feel young and bold!
Wonder if they'd go away
If I went outside to play
Maybe not, but what the heck
At least inside I'm not a wreck!

Taking the time to compose those silly lines proved to be a breakthrough moment as it reminded me that the "little lines that creep across my face like vines" are not really wrinkles -- but something worth crowing about: LAUGH LINES!

But it wasn't until my mega-talented youngest sister, Mary Hauprich Reilly, surprised me by bringing Steve's old cover cartoon to life for a computer animation class she was taking at college earlier this year that things really kicked into high gear. When I saw how Mary had made Little Annie Looney shuffle across the floor in those fuzzy slippers and then leap high in the air to do a split, I collapsed into fits of glorious sidesplitting giggles as did everyone else who viewed Mary's creative offering -- which, by the way, earned her an "A."

I knew the time had come to finish what I'd started several years earlier. To finish writing a book about the laugh lines behind the bylines that had accompanied stories I'd written over the years. Best of all, I knew my own funny bone wasn't broken, but merely fractured. It could, should and would be fixed and put to good use again! I hope you'll agree that it has been . . . lest I resign myself to being a has-been writer doomed to reciting ridiculous limericks as I wipe even more egg off of my face.

Please note that the first eight segments are reprints of light-hearted essays which appeared in the original version of this book. Because of certain transitions since those passages were crafted in the 1990s, a few minor modifications have been made and some fillers and/or footnotes added where appropriate. All other text is exactly as it was printed around the turn-of-the-millennium. May we all live happily ever LAUGHTER!

16

Deep laugh lines
have deep roots

What came BEFORE
the chicken on my shoulder
and the egg on my face!

How growing up in a "Happier by the Dozen" household planted seeds for getting the most "smileage" out of life!

Big families like the one immortalized in "Cheaper By The Dozen" are going the way of the dinosaur. One has to search long and hard these days to find a young family with more than four children. Those with five or six offspring are looked upon with awe while those with over seven probably qualify for some sort of endangered species list!

What, if anything, are today's smaller families missing out on?

Here's what author Ann Hauprich and brother Francis came up with when they sat down to reminisce about their early years as fourth and fifth, respectively, in a line of 10 siblings.

Growing up in a household with 10 children meant never having to sit on a cold toilet seat. It meant expecting to get a busy signal whenever you phoned home and not really minding being sent to your room since someone else was probably already there.

It meant learning at an early age how to divide a gallon of ice cream into 12 even portions and multiplying recipes by at least three or four. It meant submitting to roll calls inside the cramped station wagon to make sure no one was inadvertently left behind, and the thrill of watching your father make a frantic U-turn upon the discovery that some slowpoke (or attention-seeker) was, indeed, missing in action.

Then there was the excitement of being part of the family's entourage of overflowing shopping carts at the grocery store, zigzagging up and down aisles in hot pursuit of bargain brands and two for one specials! Those who remained at home were expected to form a line of bag hustlers to quickly transport perishables from the car to the fridge and freezer.

These, at least, are some of our more vivid memories of being part of a Baby Boom household back in the '60s.

Like so many other Roman Catholics of that era, our parents were firm believers in child control as opposed to birth control. Or, some might argue, they were advocates of Planned Parenthood of another sort: they planned to have lots of children and they got them!

In those days, no one blinked an eye as we paraded down the aisle of St. Ambrose Church in Latham, New York in our best Sunday hand-me-downs. Occasionally, we were reduced to the size of a little league baseball team when our eldest brother, Tim, donned cassock and surplice to serve on the altar. Of course, we weren't the only family to occupy an entire pew.

The Kopachs, for instance, outnumbered us by one or two (we kids used to "keep score" -- as though there was a contest over who would wind up with the most sisters and brothers.) Let's just say the neighborhood was literally crawling with examples of the Cheaper By The Dozen phenomenon.

Unfortunately, we lost count of which family was "winning" the biggest family competition after our "Gang of 12" moved to more spacious upstate quarters in the late '60s. But we never forgot St. Ambrose -- and it's quite possible the nuns threw a party celebrating the extra filing cabinet space when our records were transferred north to Ballston Spa!

As students in a Catholic elementary school, it was frequently the case that a teacher with several years at the same grade level would have one family member after the next -- and would invariably call on us using another sibling's name.

Occasionally, one got the distinct impression that "Big Sister" was watching as the nuns called an older sibling on the carpet for the transgressions of a younger one.

A case in point was when firstborn Charlene was summoned to the principal's office to sew a severed seat in the uniform slacks of accident prone brother, Tim. With oversized needle and thick, dark thread in hand, Charlene sat in the girl's lavatory stitching Tim's britches while he sulked in humiliation in the nearby boys' washroom.

The used book policy meant you had a whole summer to get sick of looking at next year's educational texts and provided ample time to creatively camouflage the previous years of sibling abuse. Even school lunches defied the norm! At one point, our "Betty Crocker-ish" mother (who later traded in her apron for a teacher's garb) grew impatient with our expressed open individuality regarding lunch menu and went on strike. The problem was rooted in personal preferences not just for grape or strawberry jam vs. jelly -- but for the thickness and texture of said contents.

Then there was the smooth vs. crunchy peanut butter conflict, those who wanted bologna with mustard vs. those who preferred it with mayonnaise, and so on. Once 20 small hands began making their own school lunches, the system fell apart completely! Names were omitted from brown bags and siblings were frequently shocked by the sight and odor of a dill pickle and mayo in place of their coveted Fluffernutter.

But only in our dreams would we unwrap thickly layered roast beef with lettuce and tomato on a sesame seed hardroll and a RingDing Junior. (Those delicacies, it seemed, were NEVER on special at the grocery store!)

At the end of the school day uniforms went flying in all directions and it was time to argue over whose turn it was to peel and mash the 24 potatoes -- or worse -- whose dish night it was! Amazing deals were negotiated around switching KP duties.

You'd pray hotdogs were on the menu if it was your dish night. If only the priest realized who was in the confessional with him, he would surely have added "cheerfully scrubbing burned casserole pans" to his roster of penance possibilities.

Of course, the guest leaf always remained intact in the dining room table -- and a card table had to be set up in another room if a school chum accepted an invitation to dine with our family.

Meanwhile, Charles Atlas muscles were developed opening industrial-sized cans of Grandma Brown's baked beans and army-surplus jars of fruit cocktail. You never left food on your plate for fear the remains would appear before you disguised as soup or goulash at the next meal. (Our parents vehemently deny this was the case; however, they're outnumbered by 10 heirs who insist "meatloaf" once consisted of one-third ground beef and two-thirds leftovers.) Our parents invented Hamburger Helper years before it was commercially marketed!

Visitors to the hectic Hauprich household on a Saturday evening might well have thought they'd taken a wrong turn and ended up at a sheep shearing demonstration. Only instead of clipping wool from the bodies of fuzzy livestock, our Dad was zealously wielding his newly purchased electric clippers up, down and all around the heads of his six sons: Tim, Frank, Bill, Steve, Chris and Andy.

While this was a considerable improvement over the technique involving a cereal bowl on the head, the resulting Punker styles were not yet in vogue. Suffice to say, the boys frequently refused to leave the house without caps on their heads following visits to Don's Scalping Salon.

Now for some families, 12 members would have been enough. But ours mushroomed to include an assortment of pets almost broad enough to rival those at the local game farm. Included over the years were wild turtles, snakes, hamsters, gerbils, birds, fish, cats, dogs and a multitude of frogs -- which at one time numbered around 40 in an old laundry tub.

The frog infestation was much akin to a Biblical plague. Fortunately for our much beleaguered parents, Smokey, one of our felines -- a "mouser" at heart -- also had a taste for frogs' legs. This cat was also a suspect in the mysterious disappearance of "Myrtle The Turtle."

Some of the pets were buried at sea (a quick flush took care of their remains) while others were ceremoniously laid to rest in a backyard plot. We had shoe boxes of every size to accommodate those dearly departed to the great animal kingdom beyond -- and we prayed that our favorite pets might someday be allowed to join us in Heaven - - despite their lack of an immortal soul!

A milestone of big family life was reached when you no longer had to rely on an older sibling for your wardrobe. In order to finance those "non-hand-me-down" clothes, however, it was necessary to take a job -- often a "hand-me-down" job that had previously belonged to an older sibling!

And what better way to commute to and from that "hand-me-down" job than in a "hand-me-down" car! The sibling transferable jobs ran the gamut from paper routes to baby-sitting assignments to cleaning to restaurant work.

Owners of a posh Saratoga Springs eating establishment never had to worry about placing a classified ad because a Hauprich had given notice. There was always a younger sibling eagerly waiting in line for the chance to earn some extra money.

In the automotive department, a car owned by third-born, Pam was the first to become a "hand-me-down" followed by a VW "bug" that started out with Tim behind the wheel and then went to Frank before being driven away by an in-law.

Perhaps the most notable of the hand-me-down cars was a `79 VW Rabbit bought new by our parents then traded to Frank and later to Mary Beth, the youngest of the Hauprich children.

At the time she assumed ownership of the vehicle, Mary was pregnant with her third baby and so was becoming nauseatingly familiar with the expression `the rabbit died.' It was a phrase that could NOT be applied to the other Rabbit in her life -- one that was still going strong with over 200,000 miles registered on the odometer!

In today's throw away society, it helps to reflect back upon our "waste not want not" roots. There was no chance of us being spoiled by material possessions. A new toy came our way once a year -- at Christmas. The rest of the year, we "recycled" one another's play things. Somehow, we didn't feel deprived. For as little as we had, our parents could always show us a child who had less, and we grew up believing it really was "more blessed to give than to receive." Thanks to our many siblings, sharing became second nature, and the luxuries our friends took for granted were genuinely appreciated and treasured in our family circle.

Yes, we had more responsibilities than those in smaller families . . . but we also had more freedoms. We weren't "mothered" to death -- just to life.

We learned to be independent at an early age. Once our chores and homework were done, our time was our own. For some, that meant drama, sports or other extracurricular activities connected with the church or school; for others it meant withdrawing to sketch or create poetry. Still others chose to experiment in the kitchen or test carpentry skills in the basement.

There was no pressure to be anyone or anything but ourselves. None of us felt a need to prove our worth. We shared the same roof with 11 other human beings who loved and accepted us -- warts and all. Even so, a sense of humor was critical to one's emotional survival. Laughter was the best medicine then -- as it is now. Only if you didn't come around on your own in those days, there were 100 or more fingers standing by just itching to tickle your funny bone! This same heritage that helped us through our formative years continues to sustain us through the challenges of our adult lives.

Whenever we need a good laugh or a cry, we need only pick up the phone to know there are still 11 "kindred spirits" ready to share our joy or pain. No matter how many miles may separate us, we feel closely knit. The fabric from which we are made may be on the brink of extinction, but the threads are strong. We're grateful to our parents for placing such a high price on life that we could count ourselves among the last of a dying breed.

As this book was going to print, Donald & Audrey Hauprich were contemplating plans for a 60th wedding anniversary celebration in 2008 and using a calculator to keep tabs on the number of grandchildren and great-grandchildren who will likely require high chairs and bibs at the event! All 10 of the couple's now adult offspring are just grateful they won't have to wash dishes by hand after the guests depart!

Nothing to crow about!

Notes on being a freelance writer & other
funny business along the publishing path

Cooped up author hatches plot to nab Pullet Surprise

There was a time in a past writing life when I enjoyed the luxury of a private office complete with a secretary to screen my calls and interrogate visitors about whether or not they had appointments. That was before I felt guilty about leaving my youngsters in day care and opted to establish an editorial consulting business in the comfort of my own home on five secluded acres in a hamlet on the outskirts of Saratoga Springs.

The downside of this arrangement was that my concentration was often broken by the sights and sounds of exuberant children interacting elsewhere in the house. "Ah well," I was known to lament as I walked away from my word processor to pinpoint the source of my latest distraction, "I guess the Pulitzer Prize will just have to wait."

Things became even more hectic during a week when the two older girls transformed our kitchen into a chicken hatchery as part of a home-schooling science project. Tara and Marietje wanted to keep the peeping chicks, but I was hesitant until Hubby (hereafter known as "Hub") mentioned some might eventually develop into fertile hens with profitable egg-laying potential. All those years of creative writing finally paid off when my brain instantly hatched this plot: "You mean I finally get my Pullet Surprise?"

Alas, it was not to be. The dozen or so baby chicks were given names like Chubbykins and Buddy -- not to mention full run of our spread. As for the eggs, rather than being transformed into those of a scrambled, poached or fried variety, they hatched into more feathered free-range friends with names like Cutie, Sweetie and Baby.

Any mention of frying, baking or broiling them or any of their kin brought responses from the girls that made us feel like we, rather than the barnyard critters, were at the bottom of the food chain! As a result, we welcomed the arrival of so many chick-ren, grandchick-ren, and great-grandchick-ren that we had to put an addition on the coop and keep a hose near our back stoop!

Guests learned the hard way to enter and exit their cars and vans in a hurry as the wind swept aroma of a single crumb on the vehicle's seat or floor quickly drew fowl visitors seeking to peck it out. Gone were the days when I carried a flashlight into the underground parking garage in the city to make sure no strangers were crouched down in the back seat. Now a broom was needed to shoo away potential stowaways before daring to get behind the wheel.

As some of the chicks were about to enter their 10th birthdays (making them well over 100 in human years) we contemplated requesting recognition for these tough old birds in the *Guinness Book of World Records* as well as drafting letters seeking "old egg pensions" to subsidize the cost of customized canes and the construction of handicapped ramps leading to the nesting boxes.

In the end, only the best laid plans would do for our once dapper flappers. These chicks truly were something to crow about. Each certainly earned a halo to go with its wings!

So this is why writers stopped using quill pens

What budding author hasn't pondered the appearance of a favorite early literary master only to find the subject posed reflectively with a quill pen in hand? Surely that is how the greats wished to be remembered by future generations contemplating the next inspired line to flow from their distinctively shaped writing instruments.

I, for one, had always assumed famous poets and novelists utilized quills that had been skillfully plucked from the wing or tail of a goose or some exotic bird. In recent years, however, I've started wondering if a few writers (especially those who managed to craft classics in more rustic surroundings) got stuck using something from a member of the Erethizontidae family.

In layman's terms: a porcupine.

That revelation came to me as my nocturnal attempts to manicure a magazine manuscript were interrupted by howls and yowls from Max, devoted family pet and home- office guard dog. Writing after dark to meet an editor's early morning electronic mail deadline, I had ruled out the possibility of being interrupted by any of the children who sometimes made it a challenge to string two coherent syllables together during the daylight hours.

Being mathematically-challenged, I'm not sure what the probability was that Max would exit the house for a call of nature in the nearby woods only to return with a quill-filled mouth. The resulting canine craziness caused the entire household to quite literally rise to the occasion, each member offering a conflicting solution to the prickly problem.

Born and raised in the heavily forested foothills of the Adirondacks, the man of the house insisted there was no need to panic -- especially if panicking involved calling a veterinarian in the wee small hours when fees tended to escalate.

"You city slickers are all alike," admonished Hub, making a reference to my suburban roots and late-blooming urban branches.

A suggestion to call 911 came from one child only to be followed by chants of "call the vet, call the vet, hurry up and call the vet," from another.

Although it pained him to see Max in pain, pajama-clad Hub needed a few minutes to figure out which would be the lesser of two weevils at such a late hour. Retrieving a calculator from his briefcase and a pair of pliers from his toolbox, he mused: "I wonder if they charge by the quill or by the hour." Could no one under four feet tall grasp how painful it was for a person raised in the country to write checks for something people used to take care of for free with a pair of pliers?

And so it went for what seemed an eternity while I reminded everyone that I was deadlocked on a deadline. To drive home the depths of my dilemma, I explained that a deadline was originally a boundary around a military prison beyond which an inmate could not venture without risk of being shot by the guards. "Now do you people understand why I take my deadlines so seriously?" I demanded.

In the end, sanity prevailed. A vet was called, an anesthetic was administered, the quills were removed and Max was contentedly chowing down on his favorite fare. His days as a quill-seeker were over, ending not with a bark-- but with a whimper.

The downside of the misadventure was that my submission wound up being less than spine-tingling and spurred my editor to make such needling remarks as "What's the point?"

And so, years from now, if by some miracle my image is included in any kind of literary reference, be sure to take a close look at the quills in my hand. There is NO DOUBT they will bear a sharp resemblance to those of a porcupine -- and I'll be demonstrating how to put them to practical use defending a deadline.

Where there's smoke . . . there's a woodstove!

One of the things that initially sparked my interest in Hub was the fact that he performed traditional Adirondack lumberjack tunes like *The Frozen Logger* and *Once More A Lumberin' Go* with such gusto.

Further fueling my desire to become better acquainted was the discovery that although Hub "logged on" to computers for a living, he was self-reliant to the point of depending 100 per cent on a wood stove for heat.

Visions of romantic evenings snuggling in front of a toasty fire were quickly extinguished, however, as I learned just how much energy it took to keep the homefires burning via this method.

Psyched as I was to help haul logs several hundred paces from the woodshed to the back door on the evening of the first frost, I desperately pleaded to "log off" such duties after temperatures plummeted to around freezing.

While pretending to be in deep hibernation sometimes worked when Hub was home, it was do or die of frostbite on the days and nights he went out-of-town on business or to play his logging songs.

The long-distance telephone wires burned with candlelight lessons on such hot topics as how to best stack the logs for optimum flame acceleration.

Terrified that the fire might go out in the middle of the night, resulting in frigid air at dawn, I would set the alarm to go off every hour or so. Trudging the long hallway from the bedroom to the living room, I'd don goggles and fire gloves and stoke the remaining coals. Then, referring to a chart as I added more wood, I'd try to recreate the geometric pattern that would yield best heating results.

Often the house filled up with smoke long before the last log was in position. By the time I was done, fly ash covered my face and clothes while smoke clouded the otherwise homey atmosphere.

Alas, there was no Fairy Godmother to rescue this real-life Cinderella! Sub-Arctic blasts swirled through the windows that had to be opened to ventilate the house and by the time the dust settled, it was wreaking havoc with the shine on my knight's armor.

The day Hub and I really began to question whether ours was a match made in heaven was a frosty afternoon when I added the correct number of logs to the smouldering remains of an existing fire inside the stove, then headed into the city with the girls to shop.

Upon our return home, I found Hub pacing outside his castle with smoke coming out of his ears and flames shooting from his mouth. (At least that's how a cartoonist might have depicted his appearance on that fiery occasion!)

In my haste to unplug appliances, check for runs in my stockings, pack extra kiddie food boxes and securely bolt all the windows, I had somehow forgotten to fully close the door on the woodstove.

Within scant hours, the smoke inside our dwelling had become so thick it was impossible to go inside without risking asphyxiation and I became a woman obsessed with arguing that black was white -- or could be again given sufficient scrubbings with chlorine bleach!

My own demeanor became more dragon-like after taking a thorough inventory and realizing just how many decorative items from tapestries to drapes to eiderdowns bear tags reading DRY CLEAN ONLY.

And while good old-fashioned elbow grease mixed with detergent might cut through most household grime, fly ash and soot are forms of dirt in a sty of their own. It took weeks before the pungent odor was gone and everything looked like new again -- or as new as anything can look once it's been heavily coated with soot.

Maybe it was the grayish cast, but the ceilings never again did look quite as high as they did before the incident.

On the bright side, I soon learned how to log on for electronic fireside chats with Mrs. Claus at the North Pole and could truly empathize with how she feels when Santa tosses his soot-covered suit in the hamper after sliding down all those chimneys each Christmas Eve.

Special thanks to "Hub"
for not hiding the matches
while I was burning the
midnight oil writing these
out-takes re: hearth & home
happenings back in the 1990s.
I'm happy to report this talented
fellow still lights up rooms
with his logging tunes . . .
tho' for some reason, he prefers
to play in smoke-free settings!

So sorry! I didn't mean to nickel & dime you, but . . .

Rushing into an early morning meeting in a Small Town America conference room, a $10 bill was handed to the perky individual manning the front desk along with hasty instructions to give the change for the $6.85 breakfast order to the coffee shop's delivery person. Not the type to nickel and dime anybody, one can only imagine the look on my face when the money middleman cheerfully handed back three one dollar bills along with the food order. Sensing my hunger for an explanation, the designated tipster quickly reminded me that the delivery person had been given "the change" -- exactly as instructed! That just so happened to amount to a nickel and a dime. What else could I do but make an emergency run to the deli to hand-deliver three one dollar bills to the youth who had made the delivery to save myself a trip to the eatery that morning.

Some really do have two left feet while others remain on their toes even when they're black & blue!

As the great-granddaughter of professional song and dance man John Tiernan, I grew up believing I'd been blessed with natural shuffle, hop, step, move-with-the-groove talent. Imagine then my chagrin when I realized while out on the town one evening that I had "two left feet." Suffice to say, I will never again purchase two identical pairs of heels simply because they're a "buy one, get another pair at a bargain price." Peckhaven Publishing's Pat Peck confides she once had a similar experience when she purchased identical shoes in different colors: one pair was black; the other was blue. One can only imagine what color Pat's face was when she made the discovery that she'd donned one of each hue on her way out the door for work one day!

Country cooking for dummies: A gourmet recipe for disaster!

Perhaps the harshest "rurality" of all following a move to country is this: If you didn't buy it at a grocery store, don't expect anyone to bring it to your door! For years I had taken it for granted that a mouth-watering pizza or "Dinner for Four" complete with egg rolls and won ton soup was like an election eve interview -- just a phone call away.

Within mere minutes of phoning the order into a restaurant, the menu items would arrive warm and ready to eat. Often the delivery person brought along paper plates, napkins and plastic cutlery, minimizing the risk of dishes cluttering up the sink following dinner.

Those who reside along remote rural routes with kitchens large enough to accommodate hoedowns must put such fantasies on the back burner and start planning each and every ideal meal well in advance as the lack of but a single ingredient can spoil the broth.

In the beginning I sometimes tried to improvise, making what I considered perfect substitutions for missing recipe items, such as replacing onion soup mix with horse radish dip and using ground cloves instead of cinnamon. Responses from family members were not always in good taste, but I ultimately developed a hide as tough as my steaks, as crusty as my door-- stopping breads and as resilient as my bounce back baked beans.

Still there were times alone with my microwave when I found myself reminiscing about those bygone days in suburbia when I could simply dash to the home of a neighbor in my fuzzy slippers to borrow such ingredients as a package of yeast, a quarter cup of lemon juice or a half teaspoon of oregano.

A country cook missing such key recipe items must not only lose the fuzzy slippers but also find some lipstick, breath mints, car keys and a wallet.

I soon learned to pad my cooking time by at least an hour to allot to impromptu emergency drives into the nearest city (several miles away) where well-stocked grocery store shelves abound.

This usually meant bumping into a friend, relative or client -- thus having the equivalent of a neighborly over the fence chat in the middle of the produce aisle before cashing in on bountiful bargains.

The problem was that in the process of conversing over the produce, I'd forget the crucial ingredient or ingredients for which I had come.

Most times, however, I'd return home announcing: "Dinner is served!" as I unveiled an assortment of attractively packaged microwave-able gourmet meals that bore little or no resemblance to anything in my cookbook filled with Blue Ribbon recipes.

"Yum, yum!" I once exclaimed after sampling the evening's selections. "Just like mother used to make . . . don't you kids think so?"

Exchanging sisterly glances, a muffled response finally came forth: "Like we would know!" Though salt had been cast upon the wound of this well-seasoned, would-be Betty Crocker, I resolved not to stew.

"Let's look on the bright side, girls. When you leave for college one day and your friends are whining about how much they miss their mother's cooking, you'll have nothing to moan about. For you, my dumplings, will be able to go to any supermarket or fast food joint, and within minutes be once again enjoying the taste of your mom's homemade meals."

It became abundantly clear that my attempts to raise honest children had succeeded, when a voice mumbled something like: "Guess it really is true. You can't miss what you never had."

Of course hope springs eternal.

Some optimistic cousins (six sisters known collectively as The Heavenly Haven Gals) recently heard of my children's plight and gifted me with a keepsake book of cherished family recipes -- including an impressive number that begin with the words NEVER FAIL.

Well at least they almost never fail.

* * *

Speaking of which, when the opportunity arises, certain household members never fail to rib me about the time I failed to heed a suggestion from a publishing associate to try to secure a cover story about Rachael Ray for my then simmering, but not yet sizzling, regional magazine.

It was shortly after the dawn of Y2K and although I'd recently interviewed and photographed The Food Network's Bobby Flay when he was doing a segment about Saratoga Springs, I'd not yet heard of Rachael Ray.

You know . . . the gorgeous gourmet from upstate New York who has her own culinary show, her own glossy magazine, her own prime time specials, has appeared on every major program from OPRAH to ET (Entertainment Tonight) . . . THAT Rachael Ray!

"Mom!" my daughters continue to exclaim when Rachael's image pops up here, there and everywhere, "how could you say no way to trying to get an interview with Rachael Ray!?"

Needless to say I've eaten those words more times than you can shake a stick -- or a rolling pin -- at!

Etiquette for entertaining stranded country couriers

On second thought, maybe it's just as well that most pizza and Chinese restaurant delivery vehicles won't deliver to homes along rural routes! It wasn't until drafting the previous chapter that I recalled the whacky winter when I perfected the art of entertaining private couriers who had become stuck in our driveway. (Rural route drivers employed by the United States Post Office knew better than to turn in!)

Easily the length of a football field, the lane leading to our front door seemed welcoming enough during the other three seasons. Coated with ice and snow, it was something out of Doctor Zhivago. Cross-country skis and snowshoes beat snow tires and chains every time when it came to making tracks that led back to the main highway rather than the nearest ditch.

Just ask those express drivers who pulled in to make a "speedy delivery" only to still be sitting behind the wheel awaiting rescue several hours later.

Years of waitressing my way through college north of the border certainly paid off on those occasions when I'd venture out to my driveway to take orders for coffee, tea or hot cocoa. "Will that be one marshmallow or two?" I'd ask politely before really breaking the ice with an offer to bring out some half-baked cookies on the side. "My kids made them, but don't worry -- I'm positive the oven temperature was high enough to kill most germs."

Producing the desired refreshments, I'd often be asked to draw a map to our home so the driver could try (yet again) to radio or call 911 for help.

The most memorable driver of a parcel delivery van (for the record, he was **NOT** a FedEx employee!) was also the most determined to move on to his next stop. In spinning his wheels at 90 mph in a frantic, but futile, attempt to escape the slippery slope we called a driveway -- not to mention our rather intimidating dog -- he managed to destroy his company vehicle when the transmission gave out in a loud bang of protest and an oily cloud of smoke. For some reason, he was never dispatched to our home again.

POST SCRIPT: Not all country deliveries are dependent upon rural route drivers or uniformed private couriers. Our family's most priceless "packages" always came via stork . . .

The Truth About False Labor

Those labor pains seem real indeed
As off to the hospital you speed.
Carefully timing contractions galore
At last you reach the maternity floor.
Better start deep breathing now
As hubby wipes sweat from his brow.
You're sure it's time to pant and scream
When into the room they wheel a machine.
To a fetal monitor they hook you up
And make you drink juice from a cup.
Suddenly contractions grind to a halt.
"Cheer up," Doc says, "it's not your fault.
This sort of thing happens all the time."
Perhaps, yet you feel less than sublime.
For there's one more humiliation yet to face
As s-l-o-w-l-y home you head in disgrace.
How on earth to face the wise old neighbor
Who predicted you were in false labor!

You'd think that a woman about to give birth to her third baby would easily be able to distinguish between true and false labor. So what was I doing being sent home from the hospital maternity ward for the second time in 48 hours, head hung in shame, uterine contractions reduced from a frenzied war dance to a slow waltz?

"Don't be embarrassed," my obstetrician was saying. "This happens a lot. Many woman think they're in labor when, in fact, the uterus is just exercising itself -- you know, warming up for the real thing."

"Warming up? Real thing?" I echoed, images of a large spandex-covered muscle performing calisthenics around my tiny, waterlogged infant.

"But, Doctor, you don't understand. Those contractions were real! By the time we left for the hospital last night, they were lasting 60 and 90 seconds and were less than five minutes apart. I had to use my breathing to get through some of them. How could they not be real?"

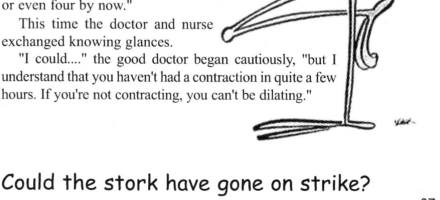

An understanding smile crept across his face. "Well, in a sense they were real. It's just that they weren't doing the job they're supposed to be doing. You were one centimeter dilated when you came in, and now, two days later, you're two centimeters dilated."

"Can't you check me again?" I pleaded like a mad woman. "Maybe I'm up to three or even four by now."

This time the doctor and nurse exchanged knowing glances.

"I could...." the good doctor began cautiously, "but I understand that you haven't had a contraction in quite a few hours. If you're not contracting, you can't be dilating."

Could the stork have gone on strike?

As a college-educated woman who had certificates verifying successful completion of a six-week childbirth preparation course and a series of related refresher classes, this explanation made perfect sense. But as a woman who had seen her hot summer due date come and go and was tired of dragging her two older children out of bed to rendezvous with Grandma and Grandpa in the middle of the night, it made no sense whatsoever!

Did this specialist with thousands of deliveries to his credit really know what he was talking about? Despite reassurances from my husband that we should give him the benefit of the doubt, I was not convinced. Clearly, one of us was losing our minds-- and I didn't want it to be me. So I made one more feeble attempt at proving not only my sanity, but also my competence as a mother-to-be.

"I've read every sentence I could find in every baby book and every magazine for expectant parents I could get my hands on. I have every chart posted on my refrigerator that tells me how to distinguish true labor from false labor, and I made sure my contractions followed all the criteria before I left for the hospital ... so tell me something: If contractions that go from being mild, 30 seconds long, and 20 minutes apart escalate to fairly intense contractions that last just over 60 seconds and occur at intervals of fewer than five minutes don't qualify as true labor, then what does?"

Matlock could not have phrased the question better. Nor could a star defense witness have had a better answer: "Often the symptoms you describe do lead to even stronger, longer contractions resulting in true, active labor and delivery. But other times, for a variety of reasons, the uterus decides to relax and labor ceases to progress. There's really no way of being sure which is happening unless you come in and get checked. Its not something we can determine over the telephone and it is better to be safe than sorry."

Nearly a week went by before I again found myself timing contractions which had been coming like clockwork at seven minute intervals for an hour and a half, and lasting from 60 to 70 seconds each, I was convinced this was "the real thing".

So was Hub. "What are you waiting for?" he inquired. "Do you want to have this baby in the car or something? Call the doctor and let's get going to the hospital. There isn't a moment to lose!"

It was around 8 p.m. as we again went speeding along bumpy country roads with pajama-clad kids in the back seat and a set of grandparents anxiously awaiting our arrival in the hospital waiting room in nearby Saratoga Springs.

"Do you think Mommy's really going to have the baby this time-- or is it another false alarm?" the little one was asking her older sister.

"This is definitely the real thing," I confidently reassured them between contractions from the front seat.

Imagine my devastation when less than a half an hour inside hospital doors, after consuming several glasses of apple juice to combat suspected dehydration, my contractions stopped completely. Even worse, an internal examination revealed that I was still only two centimeters dilated-- the same as I had been seven days earlier.

It was more than I could bear. I felt a lump building up in my throat as my eyes filled, and then overflowed with tears. Before long I was sobbing inconsolably. This simply could NOT be happening.

The nurse and obstetrician-on-call who were witnessing this pitiful display of emotion tried their best to cheer me up. "Don't worry," joked the doctor. "You can still come back eight more times before we take you out back and shoot you."

I'd like to say I howled with laughter along with Hub as I struggled to remove yet another temporary hospital wristband and fetal monitoring belt, but my once gargantuan sense of humor had shrunk with each contraction.

As I looked at my once petite body -- still only five feet in height, but now a full four feet in circumference -- I was struck with the irony that such an enormous belly could no longer produce a belly laugh.

A new ultrasound had revealed that our baby at just over 39 weeks gestation was approximately nine pounds, and I began having nightmares of delivering an Arnold Schwarzenegger sized bundle.

The baby's size and age, plus the severe swelling in my hands and feet, finally prompted my obstetrician to schedule an appointment to induce labor. The appointment was set for 8 a.m. sharp on Saturday, August 14, 1993 -- and I was determined that I would keep it.

Nothing, but nothing, would tempt me to make another mad dash for the maternity ward only to be sent packing without my baby. No matter how strong any contractions might be over the next 24 hours, I vowed to ignore them.

And so it was that on the evening of Friday the 13th, I put my feet up and ignored contraction after contraction -- even telling the expectant father to go ahead and report to work when a call came in for a computer repair around 9 p.m.

"Don't worry," I said, attempting to pry my chin out of my chest.

"These contractions are nothing but false labor. The baby is NOT coming tonight. Please go ahead and fix the computer so you won't have to go in to work in the morning when labor is being induced." Ironically, despite the constant contractions, and lack of a car in his absence, I was not worried.

As I kissed Tara and Marietje good-night, I assured them they would NOT be awakened and taken on another wild goose chase in the middle of the night. Instead, they would be awakened at 7 a.m. and driven to a neighbor's house where they could watch Saturday morning cartoons while their little brother or sister was being chemically encouraged to make his/ her belated debut.

It was near midnight when Hub dragged into the bedroom, exhausted from what had amounted to a 16-hour work day. "I'm so glad I don't have to worry about going into the hospital tonight," he moaned as he collapsed on the waterbed. Within minutes, he was snoring loudly. My sleep was not as blissful. Although my contractions were far from excruciating, they could certainly not be ignored. Careful not to wake my weary spouse, I got up and began pacing the living room and kitchen floors, telling myself over and over: "Stay calm. You are not in labor. You are not in labor. You're probably just dehydrated again. Just drink some apple juice and the contractions will stop."

Even though I made a deliberate point of NOT timing my contractions, I found myself doing my breathing and effleurage as I paced. Perhaps I had developed an immunity to apple juice. It certainly wasn't as effective in stopping the contractions as it had been in the hospital.

Then it hit me. "A shower ... of course, a shower!" I exclaimed. "Why didn't I think of it sooner? I'll just take a long, relaxing shower and the contractions will stop for sure!" As I stood struggling to wrap a bath towel around my rotund tummy, Hub made a surprise appearance. "What's going on?" he demanded. "You're not in labor, are you?"

"I'm not sure," I replied, hesitantly. He took a longer look at me.

"Oh, my GOD!" he exclaimed. "You ARE in labor. I can SEE it! You'd better call the doctor!"

"No!" I insisted. "The induction is scheduled for 8 a.m.-- that's less than four hours away. I can make it. I've GOT to make it. I am NOT going to the hospital before then. If I do, the contractions will stop as they always do. And when that happens, I'll just die."

At Hub's insistence, I finally picked up the phone and asked my obstetrician's answering machine to page him.

Apologetically, I described my symptoms, and asked whether he thought I should wait until morning -- or at least until I could no longer walk and talk between contractions -- before reporting to the hospital. "No," he replied. "I think you'd better head over there now. I'll meet you there." I awakened the girls and bundled them up for yet another moonlit car ride, leaving Hub to call our neighbor and ask if the girls might come a few hours early. "What if you don't have the baby again, Mommy?" one of them wailed.

"I can guarantee you, your mother WILL have the baby this time -- one way or the other," Hub replied. "If the baby doesn't come out on his own, the doctors will find a way to make him come out in the morning."

The contractions were now so intense, NOTHING BUT NOTHING could reverse the process. "Oh, yes," I reminisced aloud: "THIS is what real contractions feel like. How could I have forgotten!?"

Thanks to excellent coaching by my partner, I breathed through long contraction after longer contraction after the longest contraction. There was no need for medication -- there was, to be truthful, not enough time through contractions for me to sufficiently catch my breath to request any. By about 7 a.m., the urge to push had become overwhelming. But there was one small problem. My doctor was nowhere to be found. (Only later did we learn that, aware of my notorious false labor record, he had stopped for a leisurely breakfast en route to the hospital.) "Don't worry, though," the nurses reassured me. "There's a qualified nurse midwife on standby down the hall."

Just then, the doctor popped his head through the door, with eyes wide as saucers as the nurses assisted him in donning his surgical mask and robe.

My membranes were promptly ruptured and, after just three pushes, at precisely 7:20 a.m. -- about half an hour before I was scheduled to be induced -- Little Miss Kiersten made her grand debut. Almost two feet long and weighing in at just over nine pounds with mounds of dark brown hair and sparkling brown eyes, she was a miracle to behold.

It wasn't long before the obstetrician who had attempted to cheer me up during my third false labor episode popped his head around the corner. Grinning broadly, and with a twinkle in his eye, he exclaimed: "Oh, good! Looks like we won't have to take you out back and shoot you after all!"

This time, I joined in the laughter, tears of joy -- and relief -- rolling down my cheeks. As her proud papa and I snuggled with her in the privacy of our room for the first time, we could agree on one thing: our dear baby was worth each and every contraction of each and every siege of labor -- both true and false!

Schooling at Mother's Knee:
Lessons in life from A to Z

While I sometimes joke that the best part of teaching one's kids at home is that it makes it easier to justify having all those "science experiments" inside the refrigerator, the fact is the experience has been among the most enriching of my life.

Like the class clown who can apply herself when necessary, I was initially so determined to make the grade as a parent- instructor that I wound up teaching and learning far more than was spelled out in the curriculum guidelines.

The homeschooling years didn't begin in earnest until two weeks after Little Miss Kiersten's birth. Too exhausted to deal with early morning country school bus pickups or homework assignments that can sometimes stretch long into the evenings, I vowed to follow the example set by the mothers of some of America's earliest inventors and political leaders. I would attempt to teach Tara, then 12, and Marietje, 6, myself.

Though not formally home schooled during her elementary school years, Kiersten ultimately picked up much through osmosis. Playing school became a regular part of her pre-kindergarten routine and the best part of my day. I especially enjoyed having a second chance at being a second grader.

A favorite subject at every grade level has been Social Studies. I mean.... the lessons become so much more meaningful when you've actually lived through many of the now 'historic' events!

I initially expected learning to be confined to Tara and Marietje's desks --or at least to the spaces I had cleared off for books at both ends of our pine kitchen table.

It didn't take long for them to show me that the whole world was our classroom and that some of the most valuable lessons can't be planned in advance -- or ever.

Like the finest Kodak moments, they just happen. My memories of them are as enduring as they are priceless.

Climbing and swinging at playgrounds, exploring nearby fields and streams, searching for colorful leaves in the fall and observing birds building nests in the spring help to recharge my batteries and provide the energy needed to write through the night when required.

Impromptu outings frequently inspire ideas for stories that generate sufficient funds to purchase admission to historical sights and museums as well as paying for such extras as swimming, sewing and art lessons.

Taking kids along to the grocery store affords ample opportunities to solve real life math problems.

When the girls were younger, we often played games as we went like: "Which is the better bargain?" and "If we add this expensive bag of cookies to the cart, will we still have enough money left to pay for everything else at the checkout counter?"

This exercise admittedly becomes more challenging when you enter the high school math years, but thanks to enrichment videos and interactive tutorial programs available on CD-ROM, computer-savvy homeschooled kids can easily end up helping their parents balance the family checkbook!

A wise person once noted that students don't care what their teachers know "unless they know that they care."

Reflecting on my life as a homeschooling mom, I realize the same holds true of parents and their offspring . . . especially as the kids enter adolescence.

Having spent as much time with me as they have, the children I've taught "at Mother's knee" know that there is much I don't know.

I don't have all the answers and I never will.

The important thing is they don't seem to care--which tells me that they really do!

FOOTNOTE: *Both Tara and Marietje have since graduated from high school with honors and gone on to college. Kiersten is being homeschooled during her middle school years. Private violin lessons and community-service activities add enrichment to her days, though one can hardly refer to her experience as "Schooling at Mother's Knee" since she is now taller than her instructor!*

Some questions that really made the grade!

Who put all the leaves back on the trees?

After spending the better part of a weekend raking leaves into piles for Tara and Marietje to jump into, I piled the girls into the car and headed in the direction of some relatives in the southern half of the state.

As we approached our destination where temperatures were a few degrees warmer than in the foothills of the Adirondacks with the result that the trees had not yet shed their foliage, a pensive look overtook then wee Marietje's face.

Remarkably inquisitive even as a pre-schooler, she was determined to solve a baffling mystery. It wasn't long before a serious voice from the back seat blurted out: "How did the people in this town put the leaves back on their trees?"

Another time, Marietje -- who at press time was earning high marks in demanding college science and math courses -- couldn't sleep until she knew why all of the planets were round.

When I failed to provide an adequate explanation by morning, she asked for a stamp so she could mail a letter to a national magazine for youngsters asking why there were no other shapes. She was sure there had to be a sound reason. Her question -- and a thorough answer by an expert in the field -- subsequently appeared in an edition of HIGHLIGHTS.

To this day, the sight of Marietje's name on that page remains one of the highlights of my early homeschooling days!

The plot thickens . . .
with apologies to Dickens

What came AFTER
I went to the woods
only to flee the forest
before dipping, slipping
& sliding into life on a lake

Why I went to the woods
. . . only to flee the forest

Every student of English literature knows why Henry David Thoreau went into the woods. Perhaps someday a teacher will challenge them to compare and contrast that famous piece with my work-in-progress tentatively titled: "Why I fled the forest."

The porcupine to whom I introduced you in the first chapter was but one of the many nocturnal neighbors who was to disturb my concentration while struggling to craft stories and headlines on deadlines in my rustic, wood-heated office.

Rubbish ransacking raccoons and the howls of hungry coyotes were the forces behind other episodes of Submission Impossible.

A midnight rendezvous between Max and a member of the notorious LePew clan (still boldly clad in those telltale black and white prison stripes) nearly drove me to design a bumper sticker that blared "RURAL WRITING STINKS."

Further quashing my desire to step outside to drink in the refreshing late night air were the hooting owls (I'm not very tall and could conceivably be mistaken for prey) and the bats who loved to spread their wings in sight of the front door. I wasn't about to investigate whether or not they carried detangler.

Daytime was definitely better.

I'd sometimes catch an early morning glimpse of a fawn on the front lawn -- but I'd be just as likely to find myself calling the local animal control authorities to report a suspected rabid animal near the backyard swing set.

And then there was the summer when the Flea Index hit record highs throughout the greater Capital Region -- but, of course, went completely off the charts out in the sticks!

As a suburbanite, I'd prided myself on having floors so clean guests could safely eat off of them. Here the roles were reversed: the carpets and linoleum threatened to feast upon my guests!

Writing under such circumstances became intolerable and so I began toying with the idea of fleeing the forest..

At first the timing seemed perfect. The kids had agreed to shoulder backpacks in city schools for a year so I could concentrate on laying the groundwork for *Saratoga Living* magazine.

Further thickening the plot was Hub's announcement that he would be leaving his city-based job of 30 years to run a computer consulting business from our residence..

It didn't take many moons before I understood why wives shout the same message from rooftops around the world following spousal retirements: "I married you for better or worse -- but not for lunch!"

Sharing a tiny, home-based office had quickly made us realize it was time to get a new lease on life. And so very much on a whim we went out on a limb and leased a spacious commercial space in the quaint Village of Ballston Spa.

It was in those pristine surroundings that I began to write the final chapter of the forerunner to this book while dining on gourmet fare that had been delivered right to my door.

Surely this was Utopia . . . a writer's paradise . . . and yet I felt the way my parents claimed they did the first time all 10 of their offspring were away from the nest on the same weekend. Legend has it Mom and Dad stood at the bottom of their staircase in their rambling Victorian home yelling: "Stop all that quiet up there!"

Although deadlines and headlines remained part of the routine in my serene, urban-office setting, I failed to encounter even one stranded courier, porcupine or child needing a hug.

Trying to concentrate under such predictable conditions proved futile and I began contemplating a new title for my unfinished manuscript: "Why I went (back) to the woods."

Or at least to a place where woodland critters were within easy shouting distance!

Somehow I think Thoreau would have approved.

Dipping, slipping & sliding into life on Saratoga Lake

Dipping into life on Saratoga Lake can be a sink or swim experience for those who are transplanted there from slick sidewalk settings during the warm weather. The words "slip and slide" might better describe those who wait to relocate until after the last docks have been brought in for the winter.

It was shortly before the glistening waterway with spectacular summer sunsets became covered with a beauty mask of ice and snow in 2004 that my three daughters and I packed the last of our worldly goods in a truck bound for a dead end street just off of Silver Beach where the honking of cars was replaced by the honking of migrating geese.

Having resided near a busy highway since taking permanent leave of the country (and some might argue my senses) early in 2001, we decided to take the plunge into the one residential setting we'd not previously experienced -- that of lakeshore living.

Things began on a high note when a property just a few steps away from the log cabin that was built in the 1930s by the father of a composer-pianist near and dear to my heart became available for occupancy. Only as temperatures plummeted did the girls and I come to the realization that we were not completely in tune with our new way of life.

Not owning a single pair of skates, snow shoes, cross-country skis or ice fishing poles, we were ill-equipped to join in the frigid air activities so many of our neighbors were clearly enjoying on or near the lake. Not that I was about to suggest bundling up and dangling a line through a hole in the frozen lake. For as cozy as the shanties appeared from the shoreline, I couldn't get a certain related story out of my head. The teller of the tale was none other than the musical master of the log cabin, who has witnessed more sunsets than just about any other resident on our side of the waterway.

Indeed, Cole Broderick took some of his first baby steps along the shores of Silver Beach in the late 1940s, and insists the sights, sounds, scents and sensations of Saratoga Lake inspired many of the original compositions that earned his four-part "Seasons of Saratoga" music collection a Critic's Choice award from Billboard. (Cool, but not the reason I ultimately fell for Cole hook, line and sinker. It was ultimately his contagious optimism and impish wit that reeled me in!)

Who would have guessed that in his youth the maestro was more like Dennis the Menace than Hans Brinker when he laced up his ice skates!

"When I look across the lake today from the deck of the cabin my dad built with his own hands in the 1930s, an overwhelming feeling of peace, comfort and joy comes over me. Saratoga Lake is my spiritual oasis; a place of healing and harmony. That's why I ultimately decided to winterize the camp and make it my year-round home," muses Cole, whose primary boyhood abode was in Albany. But when he was a lad, well . . . some of the people who came to visit his parents on the lake considered him a pain in the padded seat because his curiosity would often get the best of him.

Specifically, Cole recalls skating out to the shanty where some of his father's Albany Spring employees were huddled and then hacking away at the frozen surface of the water surrounding the ice fishing hut hoping to find out whether or not it would float! Luckily, Cole's late parents, Mildred (Mim) and Edward Broderick, who began coming to the lake in search of rest and relaxation back in the 1920s, knew just how to reel in the youngest of the of their four offspring when he got out of line. All of the ice fishermen made it back to work in Albany the next day and Cole wasted no time in putting his imagination and his hands to work jazzing up songs on the piano.

To this day, Cole -- who is a classically trained pianist -- continues to compose on an upright in a room with a huge picture window that provides panoramic views of the historic waterway.

For many decades, the knotty pine interior of the Broderick clan's camp was finished exclusively with items crafted by Cole's father during the Depression -- from the dining room set with a hutch right down to the bedroom dressers, bunks, desks and bookcases. Two of the pieces of furniture -- one a rocker, the other a sturdy upright model -- have garnered so many compliments from guests over the years that Cole recently decided to seek to patent them as The Saratoga Lake Chairs. Before I knew it, I was rocking 'round the clock designing brochures to introduce the line of furniture hand-crafted from knotty pine with backs and seats of woven hemp rope.

51

I couldn't resist urging prospective clients to "Be the first on your dock" to own such a rare chair. My computer-savvy sister, Mary, was also soon hooked on promoting the chairs that are so comfortable, they feel like old friends. The mere notion of taking on such an ocean of a project might have made others seasick. Not Mary. This already on-the-go, in-the-know, happily married mother of four soon found herself designing a web site in between college classes and otherwise multi-tasking in and around her abode overlooking Burden Lake -- about an hour's drive from here.

Having gotten our feet wet together on the Saratoga Lake furniture project and a new web site for my Rotary Club, Mary and I made a pact to take our Sister Act on the road. We'd get a lot more done in a day if only we could paddle kayaks between our respective lake side home offices rather than fighting traffic on highways, but we've upgraded from the "shell phones" (walkie talkies) we used on beaches as kids to full-fledged cellular models. Now we can catch up on the latest family news at the same time we catch up on the latest adventures of "Lost In (Cyber) Space."

There's certainly never a dull moment in either of our domains. In fact, after years of being kidded by my mother that my life would have inspired perpetual "I Love Lucy" scripts, I'm finally starting to resemble the star for whom the show was named. While not the sort of thing I would have wished upon a star to receive, the high iron content in the well water I use to wash my hair has transformed my wavy locks from mud turtle brown to a rust-tinged mop. (Obviously the cover photo of me was snapped before taking the lake side living plunge.) On the bright side, I've come up with a slogan for a not-as-yet-on-the-market product: "Hate that gray? IRON it away!"

Cole, meanwhile, is becoming more like Ricky -- performing regularly at Chez Sophie, the fabulous French bistro inside The Saratoga Hotel in the heart of The Spa City -- as well as in settings where couples can dance the night away to some of the tunes found on his jazz quartet's recordings and those on his new solo release. Titled "In A Dream," it is easy to spot because it features a dreamy scene of a Saratoga Lake sunset on its cover.

The picture is extra special to me because it was captured for posterity by my youngest as she was trying to decide whether or not she was happy that her chlorine-shocked backyard swimming pool had been replaced by a fish-filled one topped with assorted water fowl. Upon getting the photo back from the lab, however, she had to agree that any way you cast your net -- or aim your camera-- you're sure to catch a bounty of amazing images when you dip, slip or slide into life on Saratoga Lake.

A serious look at laughing matters

Are you
getting the most
SMILEAGE
out of life?

Dr. Goodman's prescription
for fractured funny bones
&
Ms. Ingram enjoys helping
others humor their stress

Laughing Matters

Dr. Goodman's prescription for fractured funny bones

Few people take the business of humor as seriously as "Laugh Doctor" Joel Goodman. "Exercising your laugh and smile muscles each day -- inner jogging -- is at least as important as exercising those in the rest of your body," grins Goodman, who has been doling out humor prescriptions for more than a quarter of a century.

Recognized worldwide for his pioneering work with The HUMOR Project, Inc., Goodman has logged untold miles bringing smiles to the faces of more than two million people across the North America as well as many parts of South America, Europe, Asia, Africa and Australia. No takers yet in Antarctica, but Goodman's pioneering work has touched and tickled the lives of tens of millions of others "in humor hot spots in between" through articles and books he has written as well as via appearances on national and international radio and TV shows.

Described as the first full-time humor educator in the world, Goodman practices what he teaches. "Humor is one of the things that keeps us human, humane and sane in the midst of sometimes inhumane and insane situations," he observes. "I see my mission as helping people get more smileage out of life." Recognized worldwide for his innovative work with The HUMOR Project, Inc., Goodman insists laughter plays a vital role in the success of many marriages and corporations and can transform even the most trying episodes into positive — or at least tolerable — experiences.

"If there's one point that's become clear in the decades since I founded The HUMOR Project, it's that our planet would be a better place if people would just lighten up and not take themselves and others so seriously — and that includes husbands and wives, parents and children. People are always saying: `Someday we'll look back on this and laugh.' My question is: `Why wait?' Why not laugh now?"

54

We're not talking major tragedies here — just simple every day annoyances like a pair of mismatched socks in the underwear drawer, a traffic jam, an annoying co-worker or a tantrum tossing toddler. It's just too easy, says Goodman, to permit negativity to transform every day molehills into volcanic mountains. "All I'm saying is if it's one of those times when you can't decide whether to laugh or cry, try laughing first. Remember: seven days without laughter make one weak."

Lord knows, Goodman and his wife Margie Ingram have had their share of "laugh or cry" moments since they first became serious (or, as Goodman would say, "became lighthearted") about one another back in the 1970s. Not surprisingly, an admiration for one another's exceptional sense of humor proved to be a strong force in the love magnet that pulled them together. The ability to seek out the laugh lines rather the fault lines has strengthened the bond between them since now young adult children Adam and Alyssa joined the family tree.

"Parenting is not easy," admits Goodman — quickly adding: "That may be the understatement of the year. The late Samuel Butler once observed that `parents are the last people on earth who ought to have children.' (However)... even though parenting and preserving the health of the family are serious endeavors, they need not be solemn ones. In fact, adding some lightness and humor can be a powerful atomic balm to maintain the family as nucleus of civilization."

It seems somehow fitting that Goodman chose New Year's Eve 1948 in the sunny state of Virginia to make his grand entrance into the world. The Goodmans later moved to Maryland where a solid humor foundation was laid for Joel and his two younger siblings, David and Susan.

"I learned the value of a humorous perspective early in my life," recalls Goodman. "My Mom, Paula, who has been my most important ongoing model of humor, showed me the way."

Whereas harmless childish antics caused most moms in the neighborhood to threaten to "crack the whip", Goodman says his mother often had to restrain herself from "cracking up" with laughter. "Her ability to see the funny side of things helped me to develop a happier, healthier perspective on life," says Goodman. This outlook proved to be an enormous asset as he made his through the University of Pennsylvania and the University of Massachusetts' Graduate School of Education. By the time he earned the academic initials Ed. D. in 1975, there was no doubt that Goodman had made the grade as both an exceptional teacher and educational consultant.

Goodman's career ultimately led him to New York State, where he won accolades for his upbeat workshops for teachers and school administrators. For a while, he seemed destined to spend his life educating educators on such topics as stress management and improving communication skills. Although he often injected humor into his seminars, the thought of dedicating an entire session to humor itself seemed, well, laughable.

It took a family health crisis — and a joke cracking Texas taxi driver named Alvin — to help Goodman realize that humor was no laughing matter. "Alvin's positive outlook as he drove me to and from visits to the hospital room in Houston where my father was facing life or death surgery really gave my spirits a lift." Weeks later, while working late to catch up on all the work he'd missed while in Texas, the thing Joel Goodman refers to as The Alvin Lightbulb went on. "The key question I couldn't stop asking myself was: Are there practical ways of bringing humor to life?"

That was 1977, and at the time, Goodman had no plans whatsoever of turning his humor hobby into a serious business. The HUMOR Project was to be but a brief experiment run on a shoestring budget. Suffice it to say the shoestring was longer and stronger than anyone imagined. Before long, Goodman was laughing his way to the bank as proprietor of a $1-million a year enterprise with a staff of eight employees and a 100-person speaker bureau. (Mind you, Goodman's generosity with his company's earnings gives a whole new meaning to the term "profit sharing." To date, The HUMOR Project has provided grants to over 250 schools, hospitals and human service agencies. The goal: to help them develop services and resources that tap into the positive power of humor.)

The author of eight books, Goodman personally oversees the editing of *Laughing Matters*, a quarterly magazine devoted to finding constructive applications for humor in daily life. He also helps Margie organize and host the annual International Humor & Creativity Conference which has drawn participants from "every hop, skip, jump and walk of life" on six continents. Past keynote speakers have included The Smothers Brothers, Steve Allen, Jack Canfield, David Hyde Pierce, Jay Leno, Yakov Smirnoff, Teri Garr and Carol Channing.

Even though Goodman takes the business of humor seriously, he continues to take himself lightly:

"Danish comedian Victor Borge wasn't really joking when he said: `A smile is the shortest distance between two people.' I see my mission as helping people get more smileage out of their lives."

HUMOResilience 101

Today's lesson deals with the serious business of humoring your stress

Remember when stress was like the weather? Everybody talked about it . . . but nobody did anything about it. How times have changed -- thanks to playful souls like Margie Ingram whose innovative research and workshops on this topic date back to the late 1970s before "stress" became a first grade spelling word! Today Margie, Director of Special Projects at The HUMOR Project (founded by her husband Dr. Joel Goodman), has plenty of opportunities to practice what she preaches about topics like "humoring stress" and "HUMOResilience." Margie, who also coordinates the International Humor, Hope and Healing Conference each year, recently took time from her busy schedule to answer some questions posed by the author. An excerpt follows:

Q: When, why and how did you decide to get serious about "humoring your stress" and helping others do the same?

A: I began working in the stress field in the late 1970s, before "stress" had become the household word that it is today. My initial interest came as I was sorting through work experiences I had where I saw stress in myself and others. The first program I offered on stress was to teachers in my old school district in Michigan. The organizers placed us in the band room, thinking that there wouldn't be much of a turnout. In fact, it was SRO (standing room only). I wasn't the only one experiencing stress on the job! At the same time, Joel was starting The HUMOR Project. After our son, Adam, was born in 1981, there was such a demand for help with his work that I joined him and began to combine my work with stress management and his work with humor. Now research is proving that there is indeed a connection between the two: humor is a great stress reducer.

HUMOResilience 101
with Margie Ingram

Q: What's been the most stressful part of your quest to convince prospective clients that it's worth investing time, energy and money in understanding and improving this aspect of their personal and/or professional lives?

A: My approach with persons who are interested in dealing with stress within their organizations is to listen to their needs, what has and has not worked to date, and their perception of what would be most helpful in working with their staff. I then design a program to meet these needs. After a thorough discussion of their situation, they often see humor as a very positive way to deal with the stresses; I create programs to look at other ways to intervene with the stresses as well.

Q: Can you provide some real-life examples of transforming stressful situations into laughing matters?

A: Sure, there have been so many that we've come across. A couple of personal situations first: The morning of my 55th birthday, I awoke feeling stress about the day (surprisingly so; I usually love birthdays). Joel's comment tickled me out of my mood: "Gee, Margie, just think of it this way. You're just going the speed limit now." Six years ago, two weeks prior to our International Humor, Hope and Healing Conference in April (a very busy time for us at work), our daughter, Alyssa, had what we thought was a bad stomach ache. Two hours, one visit to her pediatrician and a visit to a surgeon later, we were admitting her to Saratoga Hospital for an emergency appendectomy. The admitting clerk had on her desk several manipulative toys; I have a strong memory of relaxing a bit as I played with those toys in the midst of the serious situation that we were facing at the most hectic time of our year. "Playing" helped me refocus my attention away from the pure stress I was experiencing.

Q: I've always loved the old saying: "Some day you'll look back on this and laugh." There's a H-U-G-E difference, however, difference between the everyday stresses of meeting deadlines or coping with a toddler's temper tantrum and the stresses associated with a serious accident, illness or sudden death in the family. What do you recommend at those times when life gets so stressful, there's simply no funny side?

58

A: I would first recommend being very gentle with yourself. In what spare time you have in the midst of the crisis, take warm baths, go for walks, call a close friend. Do those things that "fill your cup" and will help bring balance to your life. When given a choice, choose a funny book to read, cartoons to browse through, or a comedy video to watch to help shift your focus, even if it is "jest" for a moment. By choosing these replenishing activities, you are helping to balance your life when you really need a break from the intensity of the immediate crisis. Once you are on the other side of the situation, you might begin to look at all that you have gone through and find some humor in the midst of it -- a funny comment someone made in the hospital, the amazing schedule that you arranged to get done what needed to get done, etc. As Steve Allen has said: "Comedy equals tragedy plus time."

Q: Another topic near and dear to your heart is that of HUMOResilience. How did your work in this field got started and why it is important to you?

A: Ah, this is an important topic to me. For about 20 years I had been helping others focus on how to deal with the stresses in their lives. While I continued to get great feedback on this work, I was aware that we were principally focusing on the negatives, on what was wrong and needed fixed, much like the paradigm of traditional psychotherapy. I began to ask myself the question: "How is it that some people seem to deal with stressful situations so smoothly while those same situations can take such a toll on others? What is it that helps some people deal with these tough situations so gracefully?" At one point, I had decided to complete my doctorate in search for answers to these questions. It was then that each of my parents became ill, Dad with congestive heart failure and Mom with her first stroke. The next three years, I traveled back and forth to Ohio helping them and "living" with resiliency rather than "studying" it. When I did begin a more thorough exploration of the field, I found an evolving body of literature on Resiliency and have been fascinated with it ever since. Currently I am taking a course with Martin Seligman from the University of Pennsylvania, studying Positive Psychology, an emerging field concentrating on a strengths-based approach to human development and counseling. I'm very excited about incorporating these powerful, researched techniques into my presentations and coaching.

Q: Some people seem to be more resilient than others. What are some qualities that "BOUNCE BACK" people have in common?

A: This is exactly the question that I asked myself. Some of the keys to resilience are having support systems in one's life, being involved in altruistic efforts (it turns out that these help us as well as the people we are helping), and scheduling in times to take care of oneself on a regular basis (relaxing time, exercising, getting enough sleep and eating well, etc.) Looking at the optimistic side of life's situations is also an effective strategy for resilience; humor is one of the most effective tools to help ourselves do this.

Q: Have there ever been times in your own life when you felt like just giving up? If so, how do you get yourself back on track?

A: Sure, there are times when I, too, have felt overwhelmed. Depending on the situation, I may allow myself a few hours to just feel down; I don't try to deny those feelings when they're appropriate to the situation. Then I concentrate on doing things that will help me get balance in my life. For instance, I have a very strong support system of friends on whom I rely; they help by listening, giving me perspective, helping me figure out what I can do to help resolve the stressful situation or helping me put my attention on a brighter side of my life. Exercise is also important to me. After several years of teaching others that this is important, I have finally been able to build regular exercise into my life. I make it a point to identify at least one positive thing that happens to me or one thing that I'm grateful for each day.

Q: What are the health benefits of "humoring your stress" and "bouncing back" from adversity?

A: Our immune systems are bolstered and the flow of stress hormones throughout our bodies is reduced. Among other effects, muscle tension is reduced, and, as Norman Cousins said, laughing is like internal jogging: our organs are massaged, and respiration and circulation are enhanced. Using humor reduces stresses in our lives, builds bridges between people, helps shift perceptions and invites learning; it also adds to the "bottom line" at work by increasing employee morale and productivity while reducing absenteeism.

Q: Does EVERYONE have the potential to develop the winning edge in these areas? Is it possible to transform a pessimist (one who seemingly thrives on stinkin' thinkin') into an optimist who inevitably finds the silver lining?

A: Yes, everyone does have the potential for a winning edge in these areas. While some of us tend naturally to be more optimistic or pessimistic, Dr. Seligman's research is showing that there are effective techniques to raise one's threshold of optimism. An example of this would be for a pessimist (possibly with the help of someone else) to consciously search for positive outcomes from previous losses in her/his life. After one job loss, for example, perhaps realizing that the next job was even more satisfying. By identifying lemonade that we have been able to make from the previous lemons in our lives, we begin to open up to the possibility that future lemons will have opportunities associated with them as well. What may feel at the time like an "unbearable problem" can be reframed to be a "challenge that can indeed be met." While this perception shift may sound simple, it can be difficult for a true pessimist; I enjoy helping individuals incorporate these shifts in their lives.

SOME "JEST FOR FUN" HOMEWORK: After interviewing Margie, I decided to give myself a playful writing assignment. The self-imposed challenge was to recall a stressful or embarrassing incident and put a positive spin on it. Once I got started, I could have kept writing for a month of Sundays, but ultimately narrowed the list to the three ticklish essay topics that follow.

HUMOR:
Don't leave home without it!

A raccoon ate my HUMOResilience homework!

The overseas holiday that almost went up
in smoke before it rose from the ashes

A near death (by mortification) experience

You can't win a spraying match with a skunk

The overseas holiday that almost went up in flames before it rose from the ashes

I was going to send this to *Ripley's Believe It Or Not*, but I doubt Mr. Ripley would believe it. I'm still trying to figure it out myself. My kids, meanwhile, cannot believe I ever actually had a vacation that involved airline tickets rather than tickets to a theme park or a petting zoo.

It was a few nights before Christmas in the year 1979 B.C. (Before Children) and, like thousands of weary souls, I was scurrying to catch a flight destined to whisk me from my work-a-day-woes as a newspaper editor to a holiday setting in Scandinavia where I had spent time as a Rotary International Exchange Student earlier in the decade.

Although I wasn't due at the airport until early evening, I had taken the day off from work to pack, do the laundry, clean the house and generally make sure everything would go smoothly. And it did. By 3 p.m. my suitcase was stuffed, locked and tagged; the place was spotless (one could safely have eaten off the floors!) and a final check showed my round trip tickets and passport to be securely tucked away inside of a plastic travel folder.

The only thing missing was my ride to the airport. While waiting and waiting and waiting for this tardy individual to arrive, I decided to toss the last kitchen garbage bag full of papers into the fireplace and then lit them with a match. While watching them go up in smoke, I noticed some other loose envelopes and junk mail lying atop a desk and decided to toss them into the inferno as well. As I grew increasingly frantic about the possibility of missing my flight out of the Toronto International Airport, I calmed myself by separating my tickets from my passport. If nothing else, I was super organized before I had kids!

At long last, my ride arrived and when asked, just before preparing for takeoff to the terminal if I was sure I had my tickets, I was insulted . . . until I reached in to a bag to produce them and came up empty! A quick search of the immaculate house came up equally empty . . . until a hand reached into the fireplace. Mere words don't do justice to the action that followed! By now the travel agency that had issued the tickets was closed for the day.

What else could I do but pack the ashen remains of my tickets inside of a clear plastic bag and take them to the Canadian Pacific Airlines window where a well-groomed gent was standing behind the counter.

The man looked skeptical when he first heard my story, and even more skeptical when I said that in my haste to make it to the airport on time, I'd left my receipt for the tickets at home. The only way to get on the flight would be to buy new tickets -- and to pay for them on the spot. I said okay and proceeded to write out travellers checks and private bank checks. I was on the brink of borrowing a tin cup to begstrangers for the balance due when the man said, "Wait a minute. Maybe we can work something out."

Calling over his supervisor, the man who will forever be my Night Clerk In Shining Armor somehow convinced the higher-ranking airline official that he believed my story and that it would be a shame for me to arrive at my overseas destination penniless.

"Keep your money," he said, now smiling broadly as he started writing out new return tickets. But he let it be known he didn't like to have ashes smudging all of the other papers in his work area and asked me to "carefully, very carefully" collect all of the ashes and soot on the counter and put them back in the bag so CP Airlines could keep them as evidence.

"If you only knew how fastidious I am," he sighed, blowing aside the ashes that flew away from me as I was cleaning.

"So am I," I insisted. "That's how this whole mess came about. I wanted my house to be spotless while I was away."

"Well," he quipped, "you certainly did a good job. But I hope you never come to houseclean for me."

We had a good laugh over that and then, as I wiped my fingers clean on my fashionable black and grey outfit, the man exclaimed: "You certainly are wearing the right colors!" It was then and there I knew I had the makings of a good column to write while on vacation and handed the man my business card while asking his name. "Well," he responded, "it's a good thing I was nice to you, isn't it?" With that, Bill Sleno closed his wicket and personally escorted me to my boarding gate where I received a warm hug, a peck on the cheek and a wish for a Merry Christmas.

In all the excitement, however, I hadn't had the opportunity to use the ladies' room and knew I couldn't wait till I got on the plane. "It'll only take a second," I promised as I dashed in the direction of the washroom only to hear a voice yell after me: "Be careful you don't flush your boarding pass down the toilet."

A near death
(by mortification)
experience

Funerals have traditionally been a somber experience in my family. To their credit, my parents began bringing me to wakes at an early age so that I would not only dress in a dignified, respectable manner -- but also behave myself accordingly.

And, for the first forty or so years of my life, I managed to blend in well with others participating in funeral services not only close to my American roots, but also in Canada and Europe.

Then came the day when I had no recourse but to bury my head in shame inside the gates of a local cemetery. At my side through it all was Hub, who was equally mortified on the day in question.

Shakespeare himself could not have written a play with greater drama or a more tragic ending.

It was with heavy hearts that we left the funeral parlor and pulled our car into the lengthy procession headed for the graveside cemetery for a truly dear family friend.

Things were uneventful until our car, the unofficial "caboose" of the funeral train, somehow got separated from the other cars. We thought for sure we'd lost our way until we saw more cars with headlights turning a nearby corner.

Although it wasn't the direction we thought we were supposed to be going, we were not about to lose sight of the procession again.

Turning into the cemetery, we at first wondered about the number of unfamiliar faces among the mourners.

Seeing that an American flag had been draped around the coffin should also have triggered some internal alarm system. I had no idea our friend (a grandmother) had ever been in the military.

"Isn't it amazing what you don't know about people until their gone!" I exclaimed in a hushed tone. "Matilda (*) must have been a WAVE or a WAC during World War Two."

And so it went as the last of the mourners took their places around the grave. Hub and I tightly squeezed in the middle of the rows of people who seemed to be giving us weird, if not downright unwelcoming, looks.

Bundling our coats tightly around us, we were determined to say our final farewells to our friend with dignity and grace no matter how unfriendly her next-of-kin might be!

And then it happened: that sinking feeling . . .

"Dearly beloved," the clergyman began, "As we gather here to bid farewell to our beloved Harold (*) . . . "

"Harold? Did he say Harold?" I asked myself. "Why in the world is he calling Matilda Harold?"

I glared up at Hub who stood a full foot taller than I as if to telepathically communicate: "Stop poking me and pay attention!"

Not usually adept at lipreading, I mercifully deciphered Hub's message on the first try.

"Wrong funeral," he mouthed with an otherwise deadpan expression.

Pausing only to pop my eyeballs back into their sockets, I could not bring myself to make direct visual contact again with Hub -- or anyone else in the solemn gathering.

Stunned silence followed as our survival instincts kicked in. This was clearly neither the time nor the place to disclose our true identities.

With the normal escape options of fight or flight ruled out, there seemed no alternative but to cover our faces with our hands.

Neither one of us knew what to say or do when the funeral director came over to personally offer words of consolation. Sometimes silence is really golden.

Just when we thought the worst was over, we looked across at our parked vehicle and realized that Hub had neglected to remove from the doors the large sign magnets which advertised his company's name and phone number.

So this is how it feels to die of humiliation!

* *The names have been changed out of respect for the dearly departed and their loved ones. Hub and I both wanted to change our names after this, too, but we were too ashamed to show our faces at the necessary wicket!*

You can't win a spraying match with a skunk!

Anyone who has ever had the misfortune of crossing paths with a skunk knows how incredibly offensive the defensive behavior of such little stinkers can be.

Ruled by instinct, skunks squirt first and don't even bother asking questions later. That's because the nocturnal critters don't lose sleep worrying about whether or not they have engaged in "foul" play.

A threat to a skunk's well-being, *whether real or perceived*, warrants the same swift and putrid penalty: being sprayed with a malodorous substance that burns the eyes and nasal cavities. Headaches, nausea and temporary blindness are common reactions.

Worse yet, because the fetid fluid from the skunk's scent glands spreads into a fine mist that can travel significant distances, those close to the intended target often wind up being harmed . . . or at the very least . . . sickened and disgusted by the attack.

Adding insult to injury, while the skunk turns and walks away smelling like a rose, those at the receiving end of the blast are left stinking to high heavens and unable to escape the stench that lingers long after the attacker's departure.

Victims typically invest much time and energy trying to clear the air, but sometimes the pungent oily spray penetrates their personal effects so deeply, it serves as a permanent reminder of the attack.

Is it then any wonder that the term "skunk" is applied to homosapiens who are obnoxious, combative, and prone to stinkin' thinkin' ?

Crossing paths with a human skunk . . . be it in your own backyard, the workplace or even while on vacation . . . is every bit as unwise as doing so with its furry, four-legged counterpart because (I've substituted a word so as not to offend any readers):

"You can't win a spraying match with a skunk."

66

But that doesn't mean you can't sniff out such stinkers and deter them from spraying in your direction.

Human skunks excel at justifying any and all assaults -- be they physical or psychological in nature. These skunks typically foul the air with accusations, insults and threats -- then turn around to ridicule and condemn the person they've attacked for "acting defensive."

So . . . no matter how great the temptation may be, do **not** allow yourself to be drawn into "a spraying match with a skunk."

Let's face it: stress builds to unhealthy levels when a skunk is present, and trying to reason with one is guaranteed to be demoralizing, degrading and exhausting. Sooner or later, the skunk's fumes will drain both your energy and your dignity.

In a bitter irony, those reacting to a skunk's attack often wind up looking as if they've contracted rabies (not surprising since skunks are often carriers of that disease!) thus providing the skunk with an excuse to send yet another nasty blast in their direction.

Far better than plugging your nose and stomping your feet after a skunk attack is to prevent such blasts from occurring in the first place.

The first step involves removing yourself (emotionally/mentally as well as physically) from the skunk's territory. Once you have departed, don't allow yourself to be drawn back into the skunk's sphere of influence.

In other words: get rid of the skunk or put it where it can do the least damage. If, despite your best efforts to distance yourself from the skunk, you think you spot it lurking in your neck of the woods or it brazenly wanders into your garden party, do not confront it. Seek professional intervention.

While not 100% skunk-proof, these defense mechanisms normally dilute the skunk's power by making the offender accountable to a higher power. It's not unusual for a skunk to be a punk. Even the biggest skunks will usually think twice before spraying in the direction of an authority figure.

Go figure!

Could it be that many a skunk is actually a punk in zebra's clothing? Only the adorably animated Pepe LePew or perhaps Stella from "Over the Hedge" can answer that with certainty!

In the meantime, your best defense may be simply to surround yourself with positive people and resources that, in essence, create an invisible fence (or force field) that deters skunks from entering your domain.

Go ahead and light those aromatherapy candles and breathe easy knowing that being the target of a skunk's blast will soon be a thing of the past!

EXTRA! EXTRA!
Read all about some extra playful souls

'Twas a blast
to interview
this fun-loving cast
of characters

It's easy to kid around
with these grown-ups!
Quite a few are pretty good at
minding their own business, too!

Bear hunting . . .
the Agnes Pompa way!

Agnes Pompa does not fit the stereotype of a foothills bear hunter.

For starters, the petite silver-haired Saratoga County businesswoman does most of her hunting while decked out in fashionable office attire.

Armed only with a checkbook or credit card, Mrs. Pompa lures out of hibernation bears of all shapes and sizes. Some wear ribbons around their necks; others are bespectacled. Still others sport hats. All are adept at giving and receiving bear hugs.

Perhaps the thing that sets Mrs. Pompa's bears apart from others in the county is that their fur is, well … not quite a match to what you'd find upon closely examining a bearskin rug! You might say they're bear-faced imposters!

Some of Mrs. Pompa's bears started life as muskrats. Others spent their formative years as members of early Twentieth Century mink, beaver, seal, sheep, squirrel or possum families as far away as Europe and Australia. What all share in common is that they went on to a second life as someone's fur coat a generation or more ago to be saved from the scrap heap by Erika Schroeder of Mutti Bears in Hudson.

Ms. Schroeder's shop is, quite literally, a happy hunting ground for customers like Mrs. Pompa, who bear witness to the adage that one is never too young or too old to be warmed by the presence of a Teddy Bear in their bedroom – or anywhere else in their home for that matter! The fact that "mutti" is a German term of endearment for "mother" says a lot about the love that goes into every stitch of the bears crafted by Ms. Schroeder.

Among the most beloved bears in Mrs. Pompa's collection – which at last count numbered well over 100 -- is named Miss Margaret in memory of her late mother, Margaret Zepko.

The fur from which Miss Margaret was sewn was originally part of the sealskin coat that Mrs. Pompa's mother wore to Mass at St. Mary's Roman Catholic Church in Ballston Spa during the cold winter months as far back as the 1930s. Mrs. Pompa has been a lifelong communicant at St. Mary's and enjoys making and donating silk flower arrangements to enhance the magnificent altar inside.

"I can still see my mother going out the door for Mass dressed in that coat. There were four of us girls, and my mother would never let any of us wear her coat -- nor would she consider giving it to any of us for fear that it would show favoritism. She was the type who, if she couldn't do for all of us wouldn't do for any of us. So there we were with one fur coat and four daughters – Mom just didn't know how to dispose of it fairly; so she left it in her closet..."

And so it was, a short time after her mother's death, that Mrs. Pompa came up with the idea of turning the beloved sealskin coat over to Ms. Schroeder so that it might be transformed into a huggable memento for all Zepko daughters. The resulting quartet of bears have since gone their separate ways, making their homes with Agnes Pompa and her sister, Anne Groski, both of Ballston Spa, and with Margaret Peterson of Virginia and Mary Bent of Corinth. Mrs. Pompa also has two brothers, Jim of South Carolina and Joe of Georgia. (A third brother, Patrick, died tragically of a cerebral hemorrhage at the age of 32.)

Each sister chose to outfit her keepsake bear a little differently – reflecting her special memories of her dear mother. Besides giving hers the very special name "Miss Margaret," Mrs. Pompa has dressed her Mutti Bear in horn-rimmed glasses and a fancy hat similar to the ones worn by her mother. Miss Margaret also sits in a miniature cane rocker reminiscent of one used by Mrs. Zepko.

Married for nearly half a century to Nelson Pompa, the late co-founder of Pompa Bros., Inc, Mrs. Pompa also loves seeking out bears for her grandchildren and their parents: Ed and Nancy Pompa and Bill and Marianne LaRoche. Who knows? At this rate, the children may grow up reciting the story of "Mama Bear, Pompa Bear, and Baby Bear!"

Ask her about her favorites in her bear family, and Mrs. Pompa finds it hard to sing the praises of one without quickly pointing out the attributes of another! "They're all different. They each have some special quality that makes them unique. I love them all."

Miss Margaret would, indeed, be proud.

Mike Fitzgerald's sweet Saratoga success story

This little piggy's named Clarence; this little piggy's Noel. This little piggy's called Holly -- and all three of them make folks jolly!

The trio in question are pink pigs who are so sweet they ended up not in a storybook, but in a Candyland of sorts that attracts children of all ages!

Weighing in at one peppermint pound is Clarence, named in honor of a man who once delivered mineral water in Saratoga Springs, while eight-ounce Noel and two-ounce Holly have names inspired by the Christmas season. All three candy critters are the creations of Mike Fitzgerald of Saratoga Sweets.

The tale of how curly-tailed Clarence, Noel and Holly came to be is a delightful one that is becoming familiar around the world thanks to combined store, catalogue and Internet sales of more than 120,000 Peppermint Pigs a year.

There was a time when holidays in Saratoga were not complete without a peppermint pig to break and share with the family on Christmas Day. The tradition, which began in the early 1800s and continued until World War II, gradually died off along with the candy-makers who had once made them.

It wasn't until the mid-1980s that Fitzgerald crafted 100 peppermint pigs at the request of the local historical society in an attempt to revive a tradition which had lapsed a half century earlier.

Fitzgerald will never forget that snowy Christmas Eve when the pigs first went on sale at his original shop on Caroline Street in downtown

Saratoga Springs. (The shop is now in nearby Clifton Park.)

"It was so amazing . . . I got to the door and there was a sea of umbrellas. The people underneath were white-haired folks in their 60s and 70s who hadn't seen a pig since their childhood. And they were just as excited as children!" The pigs were gone in 15 minutes.

Today the tradition of the Peppermint Pig lives on, thanks to a sweet candy-maker who cared enough to bring a lost art -- and a beloved tradition -- back to the people. So popular are the Three Little (Peppermint) Pigs, that an elaborate costume has been acquired so a mascot can make public appearances and sign an occasional autograph on their behalf.

Although you can't buy a Peppermint Pig or Fitzgerald's wonderful homemade sugarplums during the warm weather, you can place orders for the holiday season and/or purchase the pigs at select outlets, such as Crafters Gallery on Broadway (in the center of Saratoga Springs) or from late autumn until early winter.

In addition to the seasonal pigs, Crafters carries a tempting line of year-round treats from Saratoga Sweets – including rich, creamy truffles, mouth-watering buttercrunch and "a paddock-full" of chocolate Saratoga novelties. If you're lucky, you may even find some bags containing "peppermint poop" -- a creative name for pink candy that "drops" on trays while crafting pigs.

Also hatched on the kitchen candy production line -- available exclusively from Crafters Gallery and Saratoga Sweets -- is a novelty: "Canfield" -- a.k.a. Saratoga's Official Chocolate Duck.

An introduction penned by Roger Goldsmith, the good-humored proprietor of Crafters Gallery, and Mike Fitzgerald accompanies each ducky confection.

It goes something like this:

In the Spring of 1998, the City of Saratoga Springs received a fine for relocating some of the excess duck population from Congress Park to private ponds. Soon thereafter, the two enterprising entrepreneurs pondered (or some might say PUN-dered) "the fowl fine" and wanted to help.

A fund-raiser was needed, so they decided to wing it. Their idea was laid before the city . . . and officials were game. Hence, Canfield (Saratoga's first and only official chocolate duck) was hatched . . ."

Originally sold to help cover the city's bill, Canfield has since become a Saratoga tradition. Whether you "pluck one piece at a time" or "quack him into many pieces," Goldsmith and Fitzgerald hope you'll enjoy the treat that turned a fowl situation into something sweet."

Zucchinis serve fun & healthy entertainment

Musical tastes may vary, but once kids sample the sounds of The Zucchini Brothers, most are hungry for more.

Dedicated to producing music that is "100% healthy and 100% fun," the never-bland band with deep Saratoga County roots uses wit to sow seeds of wisdom in the fertile minds of young audiences.

Corny costumes and crops of props further spice up the appeal of the award-winning group that has been dubbed "The Beatles of Kids' Music."

Under exactly what conditions Zucchini Brothers Jack, Sam and Steve were cultivated is information that is guarded like an old family recipe.

"We tell the kids who come to our concerts that our mother was a Summer Squash and our father was a Cabbage Patch Kid and that we are brothers in music," explains keyboard player Steve. Jack must have consumed a lot of string beans since he sprouted into a guitarist while Sam beat a path to the drums.

Each band member serves up zesty vocals (tomato juice in the baby bottles, perhaps?) and has grown a distinctive "stage personality" that can be picked out from the others on the band's nationally syndicated radio show which has been picked up by XM Satellite Radio (an option found in most newer cars) on their XM Kids channel.

Broadcast weekly, *The Zucchini Brothers, Live! At The Clubhouse* invites listeners to spend a half-hour in ZucchiniLand as Jack, Sam and Steve serve up a stir-fry of jokes, anecdotes, daily chores, and, of a smorgasbord of hoe-tappin' music!

Modeled on old-time radio, the entertaining and educational program also showcases the talents of Susan Meyer. Renowned for their work in schools, theaters and festivals from sea to shining sea, The Zucchini Brothers also make numerous television appearances each year.

Winners of the NAPPA Gold Award and the Parents' Choice Gold Award, the Zucchini Brothers have received critical acclaim for their albums *In Your Garden, Live! At The Clubhouse, Safe & Sound,* and their collection of music videos -- some of which feature familiar Saratoga County faces and places.

In addition, their wonderfully creative web site offers a bounty of silly songs and rainy day activities as well as an e-store stocked with everything from posters and recordings to comfortable clothing. A free newsletter packed with stories, recipes, and, of course, the latest news from *ZucchiniLand* can also be secured via the band's web site.

Banded together since 1990, The Zucchini Brothers clearly make the grade with educators who invite the band to play at hundreds of schools throughout the USA each year. The fact that Jack, Sam and Steve are themselves certified teachers may be one reason they get top marks in the form of rave reviews from elementary school administrators and instructors as well as students!

To their extra credit, band members have written music to go along with curriculum for grades K - 6. "The focus," explains Steve, "is on health, self-esteem, and the environment."

In other words, The Zucchini s believe that if you take care of yourself (health), and feel good about yourself (self-esteem), you'll take better care of the world around you (your environment). Programs can also be tailored to fit a specific topic or theme, such as respect, sharing or the Parents As Reading Partners (PARP) program.

Assemblies are designed for specific elementary school age groups. One program targets grades K- 2; another program with different music appeals to students in grades 3 - 6. All school programs encourage audience participation and include lots of singing and fun learning! Jack and Steve Zucchini also offer songwriting workshops in classrooms. Students choose a topic, brainstorm for ideas, and write and record their own original song -- all in about an hour.

A foot-tapping footnote: The Zucchinis are NOT your standard fare.

As a critic for the *Woodstock Times* once observed: "There's the jazzy, the funky and the twangy. There's rock, rap and reggae. And, of course, tweaks of knowledge that Confucius never shared: If you drink a lot of soda, you might exploda."

Our advice: Dig in and sample some Zucchini for yourself. Chances are you'll want seconds . . . or, what-the-heck-onds . . . maybe thirds!

British actor steals show on American battlefield

British actor Howard Burnham gets a real charge out of telling Americans the character he portrays in Revolutionary War skits and reenactments is "the man who made your independence possible."

The funny thing is that neither General George Washington nor General Phillip Schuyler would have been caught dead wearing the authentic-looking military uniform Burham dons for his performances.

That's because the famous figure Burnham brings to life is not anyone history books on this side of the Atlantic portray as a hero. Rather, his specialty is delighting audiences with comedic and dramatic portrayals of General John Burgoyne -- the flamboyant Redcoat who led the English forces against the colonists in the battles that marked the turning point of the American Revolution.

Burnham, who is also an accomplished playwright and scholar, offers an encounter with "Gentleman Johnny" Burgoyne, and what might be dubbed his misadventures during the Northern Campaign that ultimately ended with the British Army's surrender in 1777 following their defeat by Patriot forces.

First invited to the Saratoga National Historical Park in Schuylerville as part of celebrations marking the 225th anniversary of the Colonial victory, Burnham has since returned to the site to present a series of performances.

In a telephone interview from his South Carolina home, Burnham (who moved to "the colonies" with his wife, Sandra, an examiner for the Royal Academy of Dance, in the late 1990s) quipped: "I view my coming to America as finding my roots in reverse. I've now spent just over five years learning to drive on the correct side of the road."

Burnham's interest in General Burgoyne stems from his lifelong interest in history (he has an advanced degree in the subject) and his 30 years as a professional educator, most notably as vice-president of a private school in England.

No wonder his writings are praised by critics as carefully researched, well written and performed with precision!

By all accounts, Burnham has developed a tremendous repertoire of monologues and dramatic readings involving General Burgoyne, whom he describes as "a flamboyant, peacock character" that is fun to portray in front of American audiences.

"Thankfully," he laughs, "they don't take prisoners." (The real life Burgoyne was taken into custody following his Saratoga County surrender.)

It soon becomes clear to those with even scant knowledge of U.S. history that Burgoyne's vanity ultimately contributed to that defeat.

"Gentleman Johnny held the American military men -- ordinary farmers and merchants, fathers and sons, who left their daily lives to battle the British -- in contempt. It would be an understatement to say he underestimated them."

While Burgoyne skits staged in and around the Saratoga National Historical Park tend to be limited to Gentleman Johnny's antics while involved in the Northern Campaign (he reportedly travelled with 30 wagons of personal goods, including the contents of a wine cellar and sufficient champagne to steel his nerves), Burnham has also developed stage-worthy material based on Burgoyne's rather theatrical career as a dramatist and poet later in life.

"Burgoyne's greatest work, *The Heiress* came out in 1786, nine years after his defeat at Saratoga. In it, his leading lady disappears after opening night. It's actually quite humorous."

Dressing for the part of Gentleman Johnny is an art form in and of itself. Burnham's wardrobe includes a genuine 18th century waistcoat decorated with irridescent beetle wings which he wears with authentic British-made period costume and accessories.

Although the costume is usually fun to wear (perfect for brisk autumn afternoons in the Schuylerville area!), Burnham recalls one hazy, hot and humid day two years ago when the normally gracious and genteel Johnny might have lost his cool.

"I was confined to a tent at the Saratoga County Fair and it got rather sticky!"

When not in costume as General Johnny, Burnham also enjoys bringing history to life in the person of Lord Cornwallis. Indeed he once did so for the British Broadcasting Corporation (BBC) as part of Granada Media's series *Brothers at War.*

Originally contacted to play Major Ferguson at Kings Mountain, Burnham says he wasn't all that disappointed when the deal fell through since "I was 20 years too old for the role, and didn't relish being shot off my horse by 11 rebel bullets." Reporting to a historic plantation location near Yorktown for the shoot, Burnham was joined by two American professional actors hired to act as General Greene and Sergeant Lamb of the 9th (who he says had a convincing Irish accent) and 10 sterling reenactors who doubled as Redcoats or continentals as the scene required.

In all, Burnham was featured as Cornwallis in eight sequences: ordering a staff officer to take a message to General O'Hara at his command tent; walking into his headquarters with guards presenting arms; complaining of lack of loyalist support; expressing his thoughts on the conduct of the war; ordering the cannon to fire with grape at Guilford Courthouse; being rescued by Sergeant Lamb at Guilford; writing to Clinton from Yorktown; and penning Cornwallis's final note to Clinton before surrender. Burnham says two of the scenes were especially exciting as he was on horseback.

"It was rather surreal as there was a Civil War reenactment going on nearby. Suddenly a captain of federal cavalry c. 1864 cantered up and offered me his horse, "Shyster." (As it happens Shyster was a retired racehorse who was so tall that Burnham needed a leg up to get on, but did not fall off the other side.)

"Luckily for me, he was really quite docile, though there was a nasty moment when the crew let off smoke charges and his ears went back and he showed the whites of his eyes. But we -- and Sergeant Lamb -- did it."

The last sequence was also memorable.

"It was shot in a wooden cabin with smoke charges under my campaign table and a crew member on the roof shovelling fullers earth through the slats to simulate dust from explosions. I was assured that the smoke and dust were organically dolphin-friendly."

Gentleman Johnny and Lord Cornwallis, no doubt, have given those working conditions their mutual seal of approval!

FOOTNOTE: It is sheer coincidence that the saga of the actor who portrays General Burgoyne starts on page 76! Anyone care to wager on the odds?

History on tap at bubbly curator's bottle museum

Shortly after meeting the National Bottle Museum's executive director in 1990, she began answering to the nickname "Bubbles" while I somehow got tagged "Troubles." Although we don't expect those nicknames to remain on tap once we're history, we hope we've solved a mystery for those who have overheard fragments of our conversations!

You could say Jan Rutland has perfected the art of preserving history in a bottle. "Old bottles are precious links to our past," asserts the bubbly executive director of the National Bottle Museum in Ballston Spa which houses 2,000 or so such fragile antiques -- each of which contains a valuable history lesson. "Awareness is growing, but many people still don't realize that antique bottles are truly priceless artifacts that can be used to help teach the histories of entire industries as well as national and world events."

Enhancing many of the displays inside the museum along the village's main drag are what collectors call "go withs" such as old advertisements, posters, broadsides, currency and other items relating to a particular era in the history of bottle manufacturing.

Because it doesn't get much play in history books, many visitors are surprised to learn that bottle making was not only America's first major industry, but also one which dictated an entire way of life for the individuals involved.

"People apprenticed for years to craft utilitarian objects by hand, and it was common for glass blowers and their families to live at the glass factory sites," notes Rutland.

In terms of local history, nearby glass factories produced sturdy containers for the world famous mineral water from Saratoga Springs. Others produced bottles (often highly decorative) for ink, milk, medicines, perfumes and a wide assortment of spirits.

Glass can, of course, be produced in all colors of the spectrum and early glassblowers knew this could be accomplished by adding certain compounds to the basic glass mixture. The results ranged from deep blues (cobalt or copper) to purple (nickel or manganese) to greens (chromium or copper) to reds (selenium, copper or gold) to browns (nickel or carbon) to yellows (iron) to opal/milk glass (tin or zinc). Examples of such vintage bottle making can also be found inside the National Bottle Museum.

Among the largest on display are those called demijohns, huge glass containers that were once used to ship or store bulk items ranging from seeds for farmers to tanning acids for the leather industry. Some of the demijohns were built into custom designed boxes or crates so they could ride safely in open railroad cars.

In addition to its many functional and ornate bottles, the museum offers displays ranging from antique marbles and paperweights and to delicate whimseys, also called end-of-the-day pieces because glassblowers, known as gaffers, usually crafted them as gifts for family and friends at the end of their shifts. From ornate vases and pitchers to fragile hats, canes and sock darners, such objets d'art are coveted by collectors around the world.

One display showcases a symphony of colors in the form of delicate violins and fiddles that were once used to hold women's cosmetic products as well as liquor and liqueurs.

Another exhibit documents the tale of glass artifacts retrieved from a 19th century privy pit. Other display cases feature early glass-making tools -- such as shears, punty rods and blowpipes. There's even a miniature replica of workers inside an early American glass factory.

In addition, museum visitors may view short videos about glass-making and browse the extensive research library which includes a variety of books and magazines relating to the history of glass and bottle collecting, the latter of which now ranks among the nation's leading pastimes.

Those who wonder aloud how a national museum ever ended up in a such a quaint little village as Ballston Spa are in for a fascinating local history lesson.

"People forget," says Rutland, "that Ballston Spa boasted the first famous spa in the northeast and that this community was once a thriving resort destination that attracted people seeking cures from its therapeutic mineral waters as they now do in Saratoga Springs."

Indeed, the bottle museum is situated directly across the street from the former site of the once world famous San Souci Hotel where offering mineral water to guests was a serious part of the prestigious hotel's image.

Yet another intriguing display inside the National Bottle Museum is an antique pharmaceutical counter complete with a prescription record book dating back to 1904. Artifacts found on or behind the counter include such things as a container for lung salve claiming to cure everything from pneumonia to pleurisy to appendicitis, piles and phthisis -- an early name for tuberculosis.

"Reading the labels on the old medicine containers produced prior to the advent of truth in advertising laws can be quite entertaining," smiles Rutland. "As a general rule, you'll find many of the so-called miracle cures contained huge amounts of alcohol."

Oh yes, in case you're wondering, the National Bottle Museum does NOT buy antique bottles.

All items on display were either donated to the facility or are there on loan by request.

So, unless you come across a genuine example of time in a bottle, it's probably best to keep your old flasks safely at home where friends and loved ones can help you uncork the history lessons each bottle inevitably contains.

* * *

TOO GOOD TO KEEP BOTTLED UP: The National Bottle Museum also operates a Museum Glassworks in the village. Since its establishment at the turn-of-the-millennium, the teaching facility has attracted many nationally acclaimed guest instructors as well as talented students from far and wide.

Bob Kovachick: Sunny with a chance of laughter

There's nothing fair-weathered about Channel 13 meteorologist Bob Kovachick. While hardly scientific, this is the most accurate personality reading available of the popular weather forecaster. "I'm the same guy off-camera as on," beams Kovachick, quipping that his even temperament is definitely more predictable than the weather in this part of the nation!

Whether being showered with questions from students in a classroom or waiting patiently in line with a cartful of groceries at his neighborhood supermarket, Kovachick remains refreshingly sunny -- no doubt a reflection on his formative years.

An only child in Port Chester, NY, Kovachick credits his parents with nurturing his interest in meteorology at an early age. "I was fortunate because my parents were supportive of my efforts to measure rainfall and chart the weather when I was only in the sixth or seventh grade. Our house was full of all kinds of thermometers, barometers and instruments for measuring precipitation. We even had a wind gauge on the roof," he laughs.

Aware that his high science grades in public high school might have led him down a different career path had his parents not been as supportive of his hobby, Kovachick makes it a point to encourage students who demonstrate a genuine interest in meteorology.

Estimating that he encounters about a dozen high school students each year who show an above-average aptitude in the field of meteorology, he is quick to warn them of the greatest occupational hazard of his career: "I tell them to forget about being a TV meteorologist unless they can stand getting yelled at when their forecasts prove to be less than 100% accurate every time!" (No kidding: Kovachick sometimes wears sunglasses and a baseball cap pulled down over his forehead when he ventures out in public after delivering a forecast that proves to be even a tiny bit flawed.)

"People get really upset if they make plans for an outdoor activity based on a prediction of a mostly sunny day only to find clouds moved in ahead of schedule," muses Kovachick. "You wouldn't believe some of the zingers I get! You try explaining that in spite of years of study and experience combined with all the technology we have today, the weather can still be unpredictable to some degree, but if it rained on their picnic or ruined their golf game, they don't want to hear it!"

On a lighter note, Kovachick jokes he "usually hears about it" from the clerks at the local grocery store after he predicts snowstorms with possible power outages. "I'll duck in to buy something and the cashiers will point to the long lines and say: 'YOU DID THIS! Thanks to your forecast, people have been stocking up on flashlight batteries and emergency supplies all day!' I tell them they should thank me for the increased sales."

Grinning sheepishly Kovachick -- who, by the way, is an avid fan of country music and sometimes sports a cowboy hat -- confides: "I actually have ulterior motives when I grocery shop. It's my way of sneaking treats into the house that you wouldn't otherwise find in the cupboards or fridge!"

Not that Kovachick needs to watch his weight. With hobbies that include not only walking and biking, but also bowling, golfing, swimming and keeping up with his two kids at local recreational areas, the seasoned meteorologist burns more than his share of calories on a given day!

"A lot of people assume I have an easy job because they only see me for a few minutes here and there during the late afternoon and evening broadcasts. What they don't realize is that at least 90 per cent of my work is preparation. You don't just get in front of the camera and start talking."

Many viewers don't realize is how much time Kovachick devotes to public appearances before he ever arrives at the studio. "I get around more than most people realize," says Kovachick, flashing his contagious smile.

Kovachick likes the fact that youngsters say exactly what's on their mind and ask questions that are to the point." One of the biggies is how much money I make. I tell them that at the end of the week, my boss tallies up the number of forecasts I got right and the number that missed the mark. If I got more right than wrong, I get paid. If not, I tell them I have to give any money I earned the week before back to the station."

So if you happen to bump into Kovachick alone or with his family in a classroom, a grocery store, a park, a playground -- or any other setting -- be sure to stop and say "Howdy!"

Just don't complain about the weather!

Map company founder needed little direction as host of Freihofer's Breadtime Stories

Leafing through an old family album a few years ago, I found myself drawn to a 1959 photo in which I was sporting a frilly party dress and a Freihofer's baking hat. In my hands was an enormous cartoon-like drawing bearing the caption: "My Freihofer SQUIGGLE."

The picture rekindled some delicious childhood memories of a popular weekday afternoon television program (Freddie Freihofer's "Breadtime Stories") and the host who had squiggled his way into thousands of young Capital Region hearts during the 50s and 60s.

Determined to find out what had become of the program's beloved host (known to legions of Baby Boomers as "Uncle Jim"), I placed some calls that led to a warm welcome inside the Burnt Hills home of Jim Fisk.

P.S. The directions he provided to his residence were excellent!

Most of those seeking direction in the great northeast have, at one time or another, unwittingly turned to "Uncle" Jim Fisk for guidance.

That's because after his days as a trailblazer in children's broadcasting ended in 1966 the squiggling storyteller made inroads on a much broader scale when he founded JIMAPCO, creators of those wonderful "Maps to swear by … not at!"

An innovator both by nature and necessity during his early days as a set designer at WRGB, Fisk was not about to loaf when his role as a friendly Freihofer delivery man drew to a close nearly 35 years ago.

"Looking back, I realize I was privileged to be a part of television in its infancy. When I got my job as a set designer at WRGB in 1945, everything was brand new. We were constantly experimenting. All of the shows were black and white and the quality of the pictures broadcast into homes was such that most of the program sets could be drawn on sheets of corrugated cardboard using nothing but black and white chalk."

Sometimes sets were essentially erased and recycled into new ones. "We worked like crazy designing and building sets in those days. It was a race just to keep up." Adding to the challenges – and excitement – was the fact that the programs, including the popular "Teenage Barn," were all live.

"There was no taping. No second chances. Viewers saw and heard everything exactly as it happened, flubs and all," recalls Fisk, flashing the contagious smile that won him legions of young fans during his decade-long stint as "The Freihofer Man."

Through it all, Fisk says, he received little direction from either the station's management or Freihofer's, the show's sponsor, who trusted him mplicitly to script and host his 15-minute children's segments from start to finish – commercials included.

After the long-running program (it had begun with a different host in 1949) went off the air in 1966, Fisk – who was still employed as a WRGB set designer – initially felt a bit lost with all the extra time on his hands. Before long, however, the man who prided himself on requiring minimal direction from his bosses found he was frequently being asked for directions from those living in, as well as visiting, the Capital Region.

"The landscape surrounding the tri-cities was changing by leaps and bounds. The burbs were exploding ... with the construction of the Northway and so many new housing developments, schools and shopping centers, it was becoming difficult for motorists to find their way around," recalls Fisk.

When attempts to locate quality up-to-date maps proved futile, Fisk began drawing them himself – sometimes on the backs of envelopes. "I have absolutely no training as a cartographer ... JIMAPCO started out as a hobby—a hobby that went bananas!"

His first official map, which became the foundation for JIMAPCO (what else would one call a map company started by a guy named Jim?), was a detailed one of Burnt Hills.

Researched by "driving every street myself" and seeking input from such diverse sources as school districts and fire departments, Fisk took the hand-drawn map, complete with points of interest, to a local printer who ran off about 2,000 copies. His first distributor was Veedor & Yelverton, a small Burnt Hills drugstore.

Before long, the former "Freihofer Man" was receiving phone calls from such big players as New York Telephone and Niagara Mohawk asking him to chart updated maps of Clifton Park and other areas.

"I knew I had a tiger by the tail, but I never dreamed JIMAPCO would become the success that it has ... it just grew like Topsy," muses Fisk, who says he was "personally involved" in the making of at least 20 maps, driving every street in Saratoga County himself to ensure detailed accuracy.

For the first 20 years, JIMAPCO ran out of Fisk's residence: first in his basement and later in a sunny upstairs room before relocating to more spacious quarters in Round Lake. The Route 9 location is also just a stone's throw from the Northway – making it more convenient for clients to find.

Some four decades after its founding, JIMAPCO's maps can be found in many national retail chains where their excellent quality, ease of use, and accurate information live up to the company slogan "Maps to swear by . . . not at!"

Today, JIMAPCO researches and maintains dozens of its own titles as well as selling and distributing hundreds more from such esteemed publishers as American Map, Delorme, Michelin, Rand McNally, and USGS.

Fisk opted to take an early retirement from JIMAPCO about eight years ago, placing his oldest son, Dave, in charge of the business. The other Fisk children, Thomas, Barbara, and Sarah, chose other paths.

"So much of the work we used to do by hand was becoming computerized and digitized. It was a whole new concept and I felt it best to bow out and make a clean break. Nowadays I go down about twice a month and take credit when things look good."

Instead of making road maps, JIMAPCO's founder is now making tracks: an upstairs area once used for JIMAPCO production today houses a spectacular model railroad display – complete with billboards promoting the map company's familiar logo and slogan!

He also builds beautiful boats that have proven their seaworthiness near his summer home on Lake George.

But that, dear readers, is another "Breadtime" story.

(P.S. Freddie, Freihofer -- we STILL think you're swell!)

86

Why baker Patty Rutland really "takes the cake"

This multi- talented entrepreneur also has a wild side . . . but you need to leave her beautiful bakery and visit her home to sample what it is! "Some people will probably think I'm nuts when they read about my hobby, but it sure beats going squirrelly from cabin fever during the wintertime!" she quips.

One might say being sworn in as the 2005 - 2006 president of the Rotary Club of Ballston Spa, New York was the icing on the leadership cake for Patricia (Patty) Rutland. Having exemplified Rotary International's "Service Above Self" motto as a member for nearly 20 years, the proprietor of The Patty-Cake Shoppe wasted no time whipping up plans for a productive year in office filling the roles of both club president and secretary.

Patty -- who also works part-time as a nurse at a home for the aged and is active in a regional organization that rehabilitates injured wildlife -- drew laughter and applause when she joked about her decision to multi-task on behalf of the service club. "I don't think this has ever been done before, but I've been secretary for so long now that by the time I trained someone else to be secretary, it would be time to take the position back," quipped Patty, who also baked and decorated a special Rotary cake for the occasion.

Clients over the years have included NYS Governor George Pataki and his predecessor Mario Cuomo. Her quest for perfection has also been rewarded with ribbons and trophies, but Patty insists the sweetest thanks of all can be found in the cards and letters she receives from satisfied clients. She was also thrilled when one of her extraordinary cakes was featured on a cover of an international trade publication.

While aware a year as a Rotary president isn't exactly a Cake Walk for anyone, the widowed mother of two is clearly one who can stand the heat no matter how hot the kitchen gets. In fact, those who claim you can't have your cake and eat it, too, have likely not yet visited this Rotary leader's showroom where couples planning receptions are cordially invited to indulge in complimentary samples before finalizing their orders.

The beautifully boxed samples are but one reason why proprietor Patty Rutland "takes the cake" (in the finest sense of the word!) when it comes to serving area clients – scores of whom have had wedding cake designs named in their honor.

Each edible work of art is carefully preserved on film prior to delivery so that its intricate decorative details can be visually savored by showroom visitors long after the actual culinary masterpiece has been enjoyed by wedding guests. Delectable labors of love from Patty's kitchen come in four main flavors: chocolate cake with chocolate Godiva liqueur filling; white cake with raspberry Chambord filling; lemon cake with lemon filling; and yellow cake with non-alcoholic raspberry filling.

"Wedding cakes have been a tradition for thousands of years and it means so much to know that those I make for newlyweds today will be part of their fondest memories – hopefully for decades to come," smiles Patty. Although a quarter of a century has passed since the talented entrepreneur started designing, baking, sculpting and decorating multi-tiered cakes, she still blushes like ... well, like a bride ... when complimented on her extraordinary confectionery craftsmanship.

"What I love most about the work I do is that I am immersed in an atmosphere of love, celebration and hope. At the time I meet couples, they radiate such promise and bliss, you just find yourself cheering for them to live happily ever after. Mine is a joyful clientele. Working with them renews my own faith and hope in the human race," beams Patty, who has been known to pick flowers from her country garden so she could more authentically duplicate their blossoms and leaves with gum paste and food coloring.

In addition to all of this, a unique R & R experience awaits critters sheltered by Patty. For example, Peter, Paul & Mary didn't have to sing for their supper when they were welcomed as the guests in her home last year – although members of the bushy-tailed trio were clearly nuts about their hostess.

That's because Patty is one of the dedicated volunteers in the region who nurses injured squirrels and other wildlife back to health before gently releasing the critters back into their natural habitats.

Thus the "R & R" offered at Patty's Brookside Road residence and at other welcoming abodes scattered throughout the foothills of the Adirondacks stands for Rescue & Rehabilitation as well as Rest & Relaxation! As members of the North Country Wild Care (NCWC), a not-for-profit established in 2001 by noted Warren County wildlife rehabilitator Molly Gallagher, the volunteers care for wildlife that has been injured or orphaned – or, in some instances, both.

Key goals are to support licensed wildlife rehabilitators (who like to be called "rehabbers") in the care of orphaned, injured and otherwise debilitated wildlife; to encourage and foster the education, licensing and training of wildlife rehabbers; to encourage cooperation and networking between wildlife R & R volunteers; to educate the public about wildlife and wildlife rehabbers; and to encourage and foster local wildlife research.

During her five years as a "rehabber", Patty has known the joys and sorrows of caring for wildlife in need of some healthy intervention. This isn't something you can just jump into," explains Patty, as she feeds a furry newcomer called Nikki with a medicine dropper.

"Not only does it take a lot of education about special handling and dietary needs, but it's also very easy to bond with these adorable little creatures. That, in turn, makes it very hard at times to say good-bye."

* * *

No wonder a little verse near & dear to Patty's heart reads as follows:

"My furs are not in storage or laying on the bed;
they're hanging on the cage doors waiting to be fed."

Perhaps Peter, Paul & Mary will have put the words to music by the time Patty finishes her spring cleaning next year!

Michael Noonan & his picture perfect dog, Tudd!

He appears to be "the picture of health" today -- and he is! But if a camera could zoom in on photographer Michael L. Noonan's life as it was two decades ago, the result would be a portrait of a young man whose very survival was on the line.

Only 32 when he suffered a life threatening stroke (in medical terms, his condition was an AVM -- short for Arterial Vascular Malformation), Michael had to undergo emergency brain surgery that included such risks as partial paralysis and vision loss.

An apprentice with noted Saratoga Springs photographer George S. Bolster at the time the tragedy struck, Michael credits "the healing power of love and humor" with expediting his recuperation. The ongoing encouragement, support and cheerfulness of his multi-talented wife, Maeve, hasn't done any harm, either!

"I kept referring to my condition as a blow out -- which conjured up images in my mind of an inner tube bursting. For some reason, this type of thing made me laugh and the more I laughed, the better I felt. I'm totally convinced that maintaining a sense of humor -- however weird at times -- along with the love and support of my family and friends is the reason I made a full and speedy recovery," beams Michael, who is also a photographic archivist whose skills include black and white portraiture, copies and reproductions in black and white and sepia tones, hand coloring, commercial photography and restorations.

Not to shift the focus, but the family portrait would not be complete without the inclusion of a canine better known throughout the greater Saratoga Region as "Tudd, The Wonder Dog" because his image has been published in so doggone many settings and situations over the years!

Forget about waiting for the annual Mutt Strut to roll around in The Spa State Park. The mere mention of visiting the mineral springs there puts a "been there, done that" expression on Tudd's face.

This is, after all, an old dog who yearns to learn new tricks. No need to beg -- just produce a biscuit and Tudd will happily rise to the occasion. While the wagging tail offers one clue that he enjoys being a subject, this "Model T" (for Tudd, natch!) actually appears to be sporting a grin, just above the hairs of his chinny-chin-chin in many of the photos.

Whether perched on the banks of the Kayaderosseros or posing as a pooch-shaped pebble in an oversized sling shot, Tudd is a scene stealer! As for the latter: please don't call the SPCA; Tudd merely appears to be ready for takeoff. Lest his master end up in the dog house, rest assured this is definitely a case where "a picture is worth a thousand words" -- but you'll need to visit Michael studio in the Old Chocolate Factory along the main drag in Ballston Spa to see for yourself.

Be sure to say hello to Tudd when you stop in.

Ooops! I beg your pardon. There's more to this tale than that. I first heard about Michael and Tudd around the turn-of-the-millennium while researching a feature article in conjunction with the 100th anniversary of the founding of the Adirondack Trust Company when I penned a sidebar about a "paws-ible" form of collateral that went along these lines:

When most people think of Adirondack Trust boosting the community's growth, they limit their counting to the bank's contributions to the Saratoga Performing Arts Center, Saratoga Springs City Center, Skidmore College and other high-profile places and causes.

While the bank is serious about the business of making money, one light-hearted story inside *With The Strength of the Adirondacks* by Field Horne proves its loan department does have a sense of humor . . . and is not afraid to use it!

Here's how one bank official told the story of a loan guaranteed by a dog: "In July 1999 while negotiating a loan with Saratoga County photographer Michael Noonan, I inquired about the sources of collateral and, after discussing the issue without resolution, he jokingly offered the guarantee of his dog, Tudd. So in response, I jokingly accepted his offer . . . the next day we had the closing, and Mr. Noonan brought the dog to the closing and, in addition, he provided a sheet of paper which carried the dog's ink-laden paw print as the dog's legal agreement to guarantee the loan. We kept it. While the dog was here, Michael got his loan proceeds and the dog received some dog biscuits."

Now there's a dog you can *really* bank on!

Ed & Maureen Lewi:
A match made
in PR heaven

Long before Maureen and Ed Lewi ever went out on a date, others were betting theirs would be a match made in heaven. What none of the matchmakers could have predicated three decades ago was that efforts to bring the young widow and widower together would ultimately have a heavenly impact on the greater Saratoga/Capital Region!

Then again, who would have dreamed that buying His & Her towels for the newlyweds -- then worlds apart in terms of their chosen career tracks -- would lead to His & Her offices inside the posh headquarters of a corporation that thrives primarily on promoting special events and tourism in upstate New York on a year-round basis?

As partners in Ed Lewi Associates in Clifton Park, the charismatic couple's client list reads like a Who's Who of mega movers and shakers in arts and entertainment, sports and fitness, industry and commerce, government and tourism, and -- perhaps not surprisingly -- high society. A quick read of the roster includes the New York Racing Association (NYRA), The Great Escape, Duncan Donuts, NCAA Fan Festivals and Albany Medical Center, the US Figure Skating Association, and the Olympic games in Lake Placid, Sarajevo and Calgary. .

Many of those Maureen and Ed have met through business situations, including socialite and philanthropist Marylou Whitney -- whose daughter, Heather, came to work for the Lewis at the XIII Olympic Winter Games in Lake Placid -- have become close personal friends over the years.

92

Even the Times-Union, where Ed was happily employed as Promotions Director for a decade before deciding to put his full energies into his own PR business, continues to retain him as a consultant for Special Events, such as the Great Northeast Home Show at The Pepsi Arena.

The odds of this happening to anyone else might fall some place between slim and nil, but then the odds of finding another entrepreneur with both Ed's winning personality and years of experience are equally scarce.

Ed credits his T-U affiliation during the 1960s and early 70s with helping him lay a solid foundation for his future enterprise. "In those days, I worked full-time for the paper and operated a PR firm on the side. It was Maureen with her strong background in accounting who helped me step back and look at things from a strictly business standpoint. One day, she pointed out that the list of clients connected to my part-time job had grown to the point where taking care of their needs could easily be a full-time job. She suggested I should consider doing PR full-time and take the T-U on as a client."

Prior to meeting, marrying and merging professional talents with Ed, Maureen had managed properties for the law office of now retired 42nd District Senator Howard Nolan. It was in that rather unlikely setting that the seeds of the couple's romance were planted. In the course of a 1974 Senate race, Nolan had expressed a desire to have Ed handle public relations for his campaign, but was told the young marketing whiz "didn't do politics." Nonetheless, Maureen recalls, her boss couldn't stop talking about Ed and kept dropping hints that the two of them should consider getting together socially. Others affiliated with the campaign tried equally hard to pique Ed's interest in Maureen.

When they were subsequently introduced at a SPAC function, Maureen viewed it purely as an opportunity to get Ed to work on the campaign for Senator Nolan. He, of course, kept insisting that he didn't do politics, but I kept badgering him until we got some free consulting advice."

To the matchmakers' great frustration, nothing newsworthy developed in the courtship department. In fact, it wasn't until Memorial Day weekend 1974 that Ed finally placed a call to Maureen's home number, expecting to leave a quick message on an answering machine. When she picked up, the conversation flowed . . . and has been going strong ever since!

Should they ever pool resources to write a book of their experiences together, chapters might include a surprising scope of adventures (and misadventures) such as the unforgettable night when pianist Andre Watts was performing with the Philadelphia Philharmonic Orchestra at SPAC.

"Marylou Whitney had donated a magnificent baby grand piano -- a Steinway -- to SPAC and we were in the wings with the Whitneys and all of the dignitaries watching the concert when one of the pedals suddenly fell off the baby grand," muses Ed.

"At this point, to everyone's amazement, Andre Watts stops paying and gets down on the floor to look for the missing pedal while the conductor, Eugene Ormandy, looks down wondering what in the world is going on."

The gala concert took a more dramatic -- or comical, depending upon the viewpoint! -- turn when the brand new Steinway was rolled off the stage and an old Baldwin that was behind the curtains was rolled onto the stage in its place.

"Ed had convinced The New York Times and other major newspapers to cover the event and Marylou was there wondering what on earth to do," recalls Maureen.

"But Ed wasn't the least bit worried. He knew what had happened was bound to make front page news in all of the major papers (which it did) and was determined to put as positive a spin on the story as possible. His policy, the key to his PR success, has always been to keep it honest and straightforward. In the end, what transpired was billed as a real show stopper!"

In another favorite story, Ed -- who at the time "wasn't into music and had never seen a ballet" brought representatives of the European press to one of George Balanchine's rehearsals. As a joke, Mr. B. told the reporters that Ed had been taking classes, and invited the PR pro to show them what he had learned. Ever the ham, Ed -- then heavier and not especially flexible -- gave an impressive demonstration that resulted in a slipped disk!

"My ballet career ended in just 10 seconds and cost me three weeks in the hospital!" he laughs.

Ed also enjoyed kidding with Merv Griffin as captured in a treasured photograph taken of the men when the talk show host was in town. "For a time, Merv owned the WPYX radio station and he and Eva Gabor came to stay with Marylou during one of her Whitney ball weekends," recalls Maureen.

"We had worked with Merv extensively through WPYX, and through the TRA in California, etc., so he and Ed had a jesting relationship."

Other fun times for the Lewis included watching their two sons, Jim and Joe, playing and eating take-out fast food with the children of several of the artists, including The Jackson Five, during SPAC rehearsals.

But it is Marylou who elicits some of the couple's fondest memories as well as enormous admiration and respect.

"Before Marylou married Sonny (C.V.) Whitney, the high society families really kept to themselves and socialized only with other prominent families when they spent their summers in Saratoga. Marylou was the one who broke that tradition and brought the community together in so many ways by including people from many different walks of life to her galas," notes Maureen.

"Until Marylou's arrival on the scene, who would have thought such a diverse cross-section of the community would have a chance to mingle with the Whitneys or big name movie and TV stars at a Saratoga social function during the racing season?"

In addition, emphasize the Lewis, Marylou has given a shot-in-the-arm to countless fund-raisers, such as those held at The Great Escape to benefit the Double "H" Hole in the Woods Ranch for critically ill children, by lending not just her financial support, but also her presence, to their causes in order to raise both public awareness and additional funds.

Last, but far from least, Ed and Maureen marvel at the socialite's willingness to try new things -- from donning fake tatoos and riding on a Harley in a parade to granting in-depth and impromptu interviews with the news media.

"Marylou has a background in show business and is simply an all-around good sport," notes Ed. "She was the first one and the only one from those old Saratoga families that knew what a sound byte was and that I could get to do anything fun -- like being featured on Lifestyles of the Rich & Famous. Marylou agreed to do it because she knew it would help put Saratoga back on the map as a first rate resort destination."

Her efforts paid off . . . with a little help, of course, from her friends at Ed Lewi Associates!

To read more about why there's so much ado about Marylou, kindly turn to page 120.

Joseph Bruchac III: Rambo in moccasins?

Upon learning that I once resided on the same street as award-winning author Joe Bruchac, people tend to envision over-the-fence chats. While it's true we enjoyed many a conversation over the years, those of a face-to-face nature inevitably entailed a drive of several miles along a stretch of land called Middle Grove Road. It was at the end of the road closest to Route 9N where Joe was most apt to be found -- often on the side with a sign for the Ndakinna Wilderness Center where I took an incredible course in wilderness survival skills. Did I mention I can now start a fire without a match?

When Joseph Bruchac begins to tell a story, it's as if a magical spell falls upon the listener. This holds true whether the audience consists of one or one thousand and one individuals.

If a tale, legend or lesson is deemed worthy of being shared with another, Bruchac will tell it so that the hearer will truly listen, remember, and, most importantly, share the gift with others.

So whether Bruchac is sitting across from the listener at a coffee table or projecting from a podium inside The Smithsonian's Discovery Theater, the impact is the same. You, the listener, are the one destined to receive, retain and pass along the knowledge --- to become a "keeper of the flame."

It is this remarkable ability to simultaneously touch human hearts and minds that sets Joe Bruchac apart from most.

For while others on the book-signing circuit frequently seem remote, as if they and their readers were galaxies apart, Bruchac bids them welcome to what might, indeed, be the threshold of a world previously unknown to them: Mother Earth through Native American eyes.

Trying to get the lifelong Greenfield Center resident to acknowledge the depth and scope of his literary fame is, shall we say, another story. Humility is a trait that international recognition has failed to shake.

When paid a compliment, Bruchac frequently responds with humor as if to deflect attention.

One memorable occasion occurred after an overly conscientious magazine writer (me!) had made Bruchac sound like Rambo in moccasins while attempting to detail his wilderness survival skills.

"I'm flattered by your description," Bruchac quipped, "but you forgot to mention that I also leap tall buildings in a single bound."

This desire for truth is genuine, though in true *Ripley's Believe It Or Not* fashion, Bruchac first captured the attention of local audiences as a member of the Adirondack Liars' Club. Members pledge to "Always tell the truth—even if you have to lie to do it!"

One might say that was when folks began to take note that this was no "Ordinary Joe."

Since those early yarn spinning days in the homes of friends and neighbors, Bruchac's work as an author and master teller of tales of Native peoples and the Northeastern woodlands has brought him across America and to other parts of the world.

By any standards, his is a success story. Bruchac's literary achievements have been featured in over 500 publications, including National Geographic, and his name appears as author or co-author of more than 50 books for children and adults.

Named by the New York Public Library as one of the nation's top juvenile authors in the 1990s, Bruchac's titles include (but are not limited to): *Dog People,* recipient of a Parents Choice Award; *The Story of the Milky Way,* winner of the *Scientific American Young Readers Book Award; and Flying with the Eagle, Racing the Great Bear,* honored with a Skipping Stones Multicultural Award.

His *Thirteen Moons on Turtle's Back* was chosen as a Notable Children's Book in the Language Arts.

In addition, Bruchac has won the New York Library Association's distinguished Knickerbocker Award for Juvenile Literature. The author has also been honored with a PEN American Center Syndicated Fiction Award, the Hope S. Dean Award for Notable Achievement in Children's Literature and many other honors.

Despite all the literary accolades, Bruchac remains as down-to-earth and true to his roots as humanly possible.

Worth noting here is that Bruchac doesn't consider himself a gifted author so much as one who has been given "a wonderful gift" which he longs to share with others. Even when writing creatively, Bruchac feels as if the inner voice he hears is not his own, but rather a voice that has been given to him. It is Bruchac's philosophy that writers must connect in a physical way with the subjects about which they are writing.

This connection, he insists, cannot be made in a cold, academic way. There's only so much you can learn from books, videos and seminars— some things you must experience first hand.

"Once you touch a physical thing or place, it is no longer just a concept, idea or abstraction," notes Bruchac.

"It becomes a reality for you—and if it's real to you, you can make it real for your readers." The reason his own stories and poems FEEL so real is that Bruchac is on intimate terms with his subject matter.

Much of Bruchac's own research takes place around campfires, at pow wows, and in the rustic woodlands where his Abenaki ancestors once roamed. The sights, sounds, scents, and sensations he describes in his works are part of what Bruchac calls his "memories in the land." His poems, novels, and short stories would not have the impact they do had he not hunted and skinned animals, cooking their meat over open fires made in the ancient way, or used the bark of trees to craft rattles. This is a man who has cleansed his body and spirit in Indian sweat lodges; slept in teepees, wigwams, and longhouses; and survived for days on wild edibles.

Nothing lifts the famous writer's spirits more than being in the company of his wife and business partner, Carol Worthen Bruchac, and their two sons, James and Jesse, co-founders of the Ndakinna Wilderness Center across the street from the family-run Greenfield Review Press.

The 6'2", 200 pound former college heavyweight wrestling champion also gets a kick out of honing his skills as a martial artist. Bruchac likely could hold his own with Rambo as he holds a Black Belt and the rank instructor in Pentjak Silat and practices Tai Chi and Kung Fu Wu Su.

Ironically, growing up in the foothills of the Adirondacks back in the 1940s, Bruchac felt no pride whatsoever in his Native American heritage. Jesse Bowman, the dark-skinned Abenaki grandfather who raised him, was determined that Bruchac (who is part Slovak) should never know about his Native roots. He believed it best to spare his grandson the stigma of being a half-breed; someone who was a part of two worlds, but belonged to neither.

Today Bruchac, who proudly bears the Onondaga name *Gahnegohheyoh*, meaning "The Good Mind," moves with remarkable ease between those dramatically contrasting worlds, enriching both in the process. His message to Natives and non-Natives is the same: "Have pride in what you are and recognize that we as human beings make ourselves. Our possibilities are not limited by what our family was or by what other people say we are."

Bruchac believes his own long, and at times painful, search for personal identity began during his days at Cornell University back in the 1960s. Because he dreamed of becoming a naturalist, Bruchac started out majoring in Wildlife Conservation. During this time, he took a creative writing course and ended up switching majors and becoming the editor of the student literary magazine. A milestone occurred when Bruchac penned "First Deer" in 1964. "I had written quite a few poems about Indians before that, but that was the first one that got published. It was pretty exciting."

That was followed soon after by the publication of "Birdfoot's Grampa"—which went on to be anthologized in over 80 books. The author's most in-depth tribute to Grampa Jesse is found in his autobiography, *Bowman's Store: A Journey to Myself*, published in 1997 by Dial Books.

Bruchac has great respect for traditional tales and is careful not to change their wording. "We should not feel free to change these stories," he says. "They were meant to be the way they are for us to learn more."

While on the road promoting his literary works, Bruchac takes advantage of the opportunity to make people more aware of their own roots.

"Wherever we are, we need to find roots in the community, and in the land that will ensure its continuance for our children. Everybody," he stresses, "has stories; everybody has culture. Everybody has ancestors. Finding your own stories is something I strongly believe in."

While Bruchac feels it is important for people to learn as much as they can about their ancestral roots, he cautions against getting too hung up on labels. "I believe our ancestry is formed not just by our ancestry but also by our connections and the knowledge that we gain as we go through life. Focus, first and foremost, on being the best human being you can."

Who said: Never the twain shall meet?

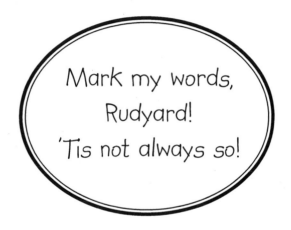

Mark my words,
Rudyard!
'Tis not always so!

David Hyde Pierce: Always a class act
More than just a few minutes with Andy Rooney
Why there's so much ado about Marylou
Mary Ann Mobley: From 90210 to 12020
Maestro Charles Dutoit & The Magic Baton

David Hyde Pierce:
Always a class act!

I was literally in stitches while working on the following story about actor David Hyde Pierce just after the turn-of-the-millennium. Having had to decline a gracious invitation to fly to Los Angeles to interview the FRASIER co-star in person because of complications involving a hysterical-ectomy, we instead let east meet west (or perhaps west met east . . . the important thing is we connected!) via the modern day marvels of phone, fax and email. Priceless photographs taken of the star during his Saratoga youth arrived via Snail Mail.

When proofs of the pages were sent his way, David gave me something better than a get well card when he wrote: "I've been out of town, so I just read the articles this morning. They're terrific, and I couldn't be happier with all your hard work. I can't thank you enough for the great Rotary piece on my dad. I played Laertes in that Kevin Kline Hamlet, and I never knew that when dad went off to war, the minister quoted the scene between Laertes and his father. You've made a grown man cry -- I hope you're happy. Best wishes, David."

Had the two of us actually met face-to-face that day, there might have been a flood as I was also moved to tears. It wasn't until a year later that I finally had the pleasure of meeting David in person when he and his three siblings made the trek to the Saratoga Spa State Park to lead a Memory Walk to raise awareness of -- and funds for -- issues involving Alzheimer's.

I don't think one could have staged the priceless photo in my album -- spontaneously snapped by Dave Sherwood -- that shows me receiving a bear hug from the beautiful soul who moments later would be leading a throng on the 2001 "Walk The Miles With Niles" event. Thanks for the memories, David. (Both Davids, actually!)

Portions of what grew like Topsy into an 18-page tribute in the Winter 2000-2001 edition of the magazine follow.

Long before David Hyde Pierce won the hearts and minds of millions around the world as Dr. Niles Crane on the hit sit-com FRASIER, he had endeared himself to legions in his hometown: Saratoga Springs, New York. Those who knew the award-winning actor in his youth recall they were as captivated by his graciousness and humility as they were with his wry wit and incredible sense of comic timing. All agree that the true measure of the star's success is that he remains as thoughtful, unpretentious, and genuinely caring as ever.

"David always was within himself a fine, fine person. I don't think he ever uttered a cross word to anyone," reminisces Flora Clements, who taught the performer when he was a fourth grader at Caroline Street School, a stone's throw from his boyhood home on Saratoga's Fifth Avenue.

"Of course, he came from an honorable family. His parents (the late George and Laura Pierce) were absolutely wonderful people and there's no doubt that David and his siblings enjoyed a warm and loving home life. It was easy for anyone to see that he was a well brought up young man, but David had other qualities that made him even more special. Everyone just loved to be around him."

For starters, Mrs. Clements says, young David was creative, resourceful, and unusually thoughtful. "He was quiet, but he was also a great contributor … he always did far more than was expected of him, yet he never expected to receive anything extra in return."

And when it came to delivering oral reports, one might say that David was in a class by himself.

"We used to assign 10 extra words, often from science and social studies lessons, to our best spellers each week and these students were expected to write a story using the more difficult vocabulary words. Well, it got to a point where we saved David's creations till last because they were so good that the class didn't want him to rush. Sometimes he'd do accents or surprise us by cleverly positioning a moustache on his upper lip while his back was momentarily turned to the class. We never knew what to expect next!"

What impressed Mrs. Clements most was that upon completing a magnificent performance, David "would quietly return to his seat wearing that same deadpan expression he uses on FRASIER. He was so unassuming that I thought he simply wasn't comfortable being in the spotlight."

For his part, David credits Mrs. Clements with encouraging him to broaden both his literary and theatrical horizons. "Mrs. Clements was great," David told *Saratoga Living* during a telephone interview from California.

"She let us tackle projects involving our special interests. I used to write plays for me and my friends to perform in front of the class, but a book I found in the school library in the fourth grade signaled a definite turning point. It contained a collection of Shakespearean plays edited for children. One was Julius Caesar, and I just fell in love with it because I got to die in front of the whole class."

In fact, David began making the whole world his stage from an incredibly early age. His dramatic debut was actually in the comfort of the suburban home he shared with his parents and older siblings Tom, Nancy, and Barbara.

"I used to practice falling down the stairs and dying which sometimes annoyed my brother and sisters. They'd say things like: 'Hey, how come we had to wash and dry the dishes after supper and David gets to clown around?' (The answer, according to David, has to do with the installation of an automatic dishwasher which freed the youngest Pierce to perfect his free-falls.) Still, no one possibly imagined that all those falls would eventually help lead to his big break on FRASIER!

"The part of Dr. Niles Crane requires me to do a lot of physical comedy, like falling, and the fact that I'm able to do it so effortlessly has come in quite handy," muses David.

There is no doubt, insists David, where he got his physical comedy talents.

"My dad was best known in Saratoga for running the George Pierce Insurance Agency, which he took over from my grandfather, Arthur J. Pierce. But my father's true love was acting. His dream as a young man was to study acting at college. However, jobs in that field were scarce during the Depression, and he was persuaded to join the family insurance business instead." It was there that David's parents met and the rest, as they say, is history.

Although George Pierce never became a full-time professional actor, he performed widely on stages in and around the Saratoga area, generating rave reviews in the process. Some of his most notable performances were given as part of the legendary Town Hall Players.

Among the most important lessons passed along to David by his father was the importance of giving one's finest performance whether or not the audience count is of epic proportions. "Dad demonstrated a genuine love of the theater that is with me to this day. The real reward in acting comes from within – knowing that you've done your best ... given your all."

Another person who had a profound influence on David's early life was the late Edith Stonequist, who gave the actor his first piano lessons – and also contributed to his harmonious outlook on life. "It didn't matter to Edith if a student was exceedingly gifted or not especially gifted as a piano player; she instilled in each of us a lifelong love of music," reflects David, quickly adding that her particular brand of humor left a lasting impression.

Young David also got a kick out of the fact that the European-born and bred private tutor, whose husband was president of Skidmore College, was a huge Mets fan. "She loved the Mets and if a piano lesson happened to land during baseball season, Edith would pretend to listen, but you knew she was absorbed in the game." In short, Edith showed David that it was A-OK to cultivate diverse interests.

Although she passed on several years ago, David says his former piano instructor remains "a vital part" of his daily life. "Edith often recommended a piano manufactured by Bluthner as a fine instrument … when I found a Bluthner in L.A. a few years ago, I immediately thought of Edith and bought the piano (which) I play every day."

Saratoga Springs music teacher Jeffrey Vredenburg is another who recognized and encouraged David's early talents. "Jeff had a significant role to play when I was in junior high. Phys Ed was not exactly my best subject, and as it was highly unlikely I would ever be recruited to play pro-football, I would sometimes sneak from the gym and head for a little rehearsal hall that had a piano," confesses David.

"Jeff caught me there one day, and to this day I thank my lucky stars that he didn't say: 'What are you doing in here? Aren't you supposed to be someplace else?' Instead he told me he thought I had talent and encouraged me to come back and play as often as I could. He even asked me if I would consider playing in his choir. Having someone like him acknowledge my talent and then giving me an opportunity to perform before my peers was a very important step. I sometimes think how differently my life might have turned out if another teacher had happened by that day and either ignored me completely or ordered me to get up from the piano and leave."

Now the director of the Saratoga Springs High School Choruses, Vredenburg vividly recalls his first meeting with the globally acclaimed actor. "I came across David playing a piece on the rehearsal hall piano and was enormously impressed by what I heard. It was clear he had great ability," says Vredenburg, adding that David went on to wow audiences by performing The Choral Fantasy—an extremely challenging piece by

Beethoven. "The Choral Fantasy is a piece composed for orchestra and piano in which the first 20 minutes consisted of David performing solo with a chorus joining at the end. It was very exciting."

Vredenburg admits he was surprised at first when he learned that David, who was accepted as a music student at Yale, switched his major to acting. "I know his parents were worried that he might have a tough time making a living in theater, but they were always a tight, very close family unit and were proud of everything he did as an actor starting with his summer stock performances. I don't see David that often now that the family home in Saratoga has been sold, but whenever he's in town, he stops by and says hello. Even though he is internationally famous, David remains close to his roots. He has followed the example set by his parents ... he is still as warm, as friendly, as funny -- and as humble -- as ever."

Similar sentiments are expressed by Benjamin Van Wye, director of the Saratoga Chamber Singers, who became acquainted musically and socially with David when the lad signed on as one of his organ pupils.

"I think David was in his early high school years and he immediately struck me as a tremendously engaging, clever, and quite precious young man," recalls Van Wye, with obvious affection. Van Wye, then organist and music director of Bethesda Episcopal Church (regularly attended by the entire Pierce family), was busy forming and directing the church choir, an elite vocal ensemble that was later to become the Saratoga Chamber Singers.

"David was immediately drawn to this group of bright, talented musicians and frequently performed as keyboard accompanist during his later high school and early college days ... for their part, the Chamber Singers admired David's uncommon musical and social sophistication."

"Even after his visits to Saratoga became necessarily brief and restricted, we all followed his career with pride although not astonishment, for even as a young man, David had been immensely entertaining and displayed a wonderfully wry sense of humor coupled with an uncanny grasp of the inherent comedy in the human condition. In those and other ways, David Hyde Pierce IS that character, Dr. Niles Crane, he portrays on television."

The fact that David Hyde Pierce cherishes the arts and music at every level further endears him to Van Wye, who through the years has remained in touch with his student-turned-celebrity and who last saw David when he directed the Saratoga Chamber Singers in a production of Gilbert and Sullivan's "Trial By Jury" at Skidmore College in which the Emmy-award-winning actor played the eccentric judge.

"It is a part requiring careful enunciation and timing and, of course, he pulled it off magnificently. It was a happy reunion, not just with the Chamber Singers, but also with members of his family. We would all love nothing more than to do something with David again, though we certainly understand that his schedule makes it difficult to do so."

Actor would have made a great teacher says Saratoga County Arts Council's Dee Sarno

Dee Sarno, executive director of the Saratoga County Arts Council, believes there are other reasons why David Hyde Pierce hasn't let superstardom go to his head. "One of the things that has kept David so genuinely humble is that he views his talent as a God-given gift . . . there is no ego there whatsoever," insists Sarno.

Even so, she adds, not everyone can bring such talent to fruition. David, Sarno is convinced, has just made it look easy. "David doesn't need a stage to shine; he lights up any area he's in. You feel vibrancy when he's around ... and I can tell you from years in theatrical circles that not many actors have that effect when they're off stage. David is the ultimate tour de force. Had he become a teacher, David would have made another wonderful contribution to the world. He would have made all of the students in his classroom feel empowered about their capabilities."

Sarno says the celebrated actor has a way of making others feel that they, too, can be funny – or profound – or whatever they yearn to be. "To be in the same room with David Hyde Pierce is sheer joy," muses Sarno, who last saw the actor perform live three years ago when he lent his talents to an arts council benefit at Skidmore College. "His generosity of heart and spirit is genuine. He has an innate wit that is infectious. David brings out the best in others around him and that's a rare and wonderful quality."

Another attribute Sarno deeply admires in David is his incredible sense of family, both his own and the community. "He loves the Saratoga Chamber Singers led by Ben Van Wye and performed with them in his youth. The Chamber Singers are one of the premiere groups in the area performing the type of music local audiences normally don't get to hear too often. David respects that talent and is wonderful about vocalizing that admiration. By continuing to share so graciously of his time, energy, and talents with the local community and applauding the work of performers at the community level, David does the grassroots artists and audiences a great service."

Composer-pianist Cole Broderick -- who earned a Critic's Choice from Billboard for his 4-CD "Seasons of Saratoga" box set -- is also quick to sing the star's praises. "David is an incredibly powerful soul with a gracious aura. When he moves, everyone in the room moves with him. Even if he had not skyrocketed to the top in show biz, David Hyde Pierce would still be a great man. Yes, he has been blessed with amazing talents, but it is the man himself who is great. . . . who he is as a human being is what truly sets him above the crowd."

How can Broderick be so sure? In addition to having an opportunity to talk with David after the Skidmore College benefit, the musician subsequently received a hand-written note from the actor thanking him for the gift of a "Seasons" CD. Included was this powerful passage: "The jazz is as cool as it is hot -- obviously Saratoga has a good influence on all aspects of the arts, from dance to theater, from Balanchine to Broderick."

Still described as having "boyish" good looks in his early 40s, David Hyde Pierce is about as in demand as an actor can be. His summer break from filming FRASIER six years earlier had been spent filming "Hot, Wet American Summer" in Pennsylvania. Other works-in-progress include doing voice-overs for two exciting new Disney animations: "Treasure Planet" and "Osmosis Jones."

Those eager to catch a glimpse of David in roles far removed from the character of Dr. Niles Crane should also be on the lookout for the Saratoga native as Mr. Kerner in "Chain of Fools" and as Michael Hastings in "Isn't She Great?" with Bette Midler.

In 1999, David provided the narrator's voice for "Mating Habits of the Earthbound Human" (with Carmen Electra) and also portrayed Perry, a deaf rehearsal pianist, in the made-for-TV movie "Jackie's Back: Portrait of a Diva." The previous year, David captivated children of all ages as the voice of Slim, the articulate animated walking stick in "A Bug's Life."

Prior to that, he wowed audiences with his riveting performance as John Dean alongside Sir Anthony Hopkins in the title role of Oliver Stone's critically acclaimed "Nixon." Yet another dimension of David's theatrical abilities surfaced when he filled the bill as Dennis Reed in the now classic romantic comedy "Sleepless in Seattle."

David's prime time TV appearances, meanwhile, go as far back as 1985 when he played a character called O'Neill in an episode of "Spenser: For Hire" and when he created the voice of Cecil Terwilliger for "The Simpsons."

By 1995, when he was better known to viewing audiences as psychiatrist Dr. Niles Crane, David hammed it up for a special anniversary spoof sketch of "Star Trek: Voyager." He also appeared as an IRS auditor who wanted to be in CATS in an episode of "Caroline in the City."

All of which begs the question: When and how did David land what most would consider that role of a lifetime on FRASIER?

It was, says David, a long and winding road the likes of which he could never have imagined when he strode across the stage at SPAC to accept his diploma from Saratoga Springs Senior High School in June of 1977.

The decision to switch his major at Yale form music to acting was, well, a major one, but by the time he earned his Bachelor's Degree in Theater Arts in 1981, many were predicting it was not a matter of if – but rather when – the glad grad known simply as David Pierce would make the whole world his stage. (Hyde, his grandmother's maiden name, was added later to avoid confusion with another actor named David Pierce.)

Degree in hand, David promptly headed for New York City, where he landed a job selling ties at Bloomingdale's while continuing his quest to grow as an actor. His first lesson: There's no such thing as a "big break" or an overnight success – nor, believes David, should there be.

"I spent 10 years in New York theaters and a variety of summer stock productions and there are just so many plays I'm proud of having been involved in. I vividly remember thinking when I was cast in Beyond Therapy, my first play on Broadway, It can't get any better than this! Then in 1990, I traveled to Russia and Japan to perform in the stage production of The Cherry Orchard with one of the great directors in western theater. Once again I said to myself: This is as good as it gets! Next came the Heidi Chronicles, a truly great Broadway production with an outstanding cast, and again I was convinced I could now die a happy man. I could not imagine it ever getting any better . . ."

Then along came a new sit-com called FRASIER. The role of Frasier's younger brother Niles was created especially for David because of his uncanny resemblance to the show's star, Kelsey Grammer, and the two enjoy a close relationship off-camera as well as on.

In real life, however, it's David's older brother Tom and two older sisters who keep him grounded.

"They're very good at making sure one doesn't get an inflated view of one's worth," he quips.

Rotarian George Hyde Pierce epitomized
Rotary's "Service Above Self" motto

On August 19, 1942, George Hyde Pierce had the distinction of being recognized as the first member of the Rotary Club of Saratoga Springs to take a leave of absence from his community service work in order to serve his country in the military during World War II.

In bidding fond farewell on behalf of the membership, club records show that congregational minister Rev. George Brock impressed upon Mr. Pierce that he was held in exceedingly high regard by his fellow Rotarians. As part of his farewell message, in which he expressed hope for Mr. Pierce's safe return, the clergyman chose to quote the advice from Polonius to his son Laertes in Shakespeare's Hamlet: *"To thine own self be true and it must follow as the night the day thou canst not then be false to any man."*

It was a verse George Pierce clearly took to heart and passed along through example to his four children as well as to members of the Rotary Club that was to be a second family to him for another half century following his honorable discharge from the Army.

Although George died in February of 1998 at the age of 87, his legacy is very much alive in the community where he exemplified Rotary International's "Service Above Self" motto. The first instance of note occurred during the Depression years when George put his dreams of becoming an actor in New York City on hold in order to help out at the Saratoga insurance business owned by his father, Arthur J. Pierce.

In a series of events rivaling those in the classic Jimmy Stewart film, *A Wonderful Life*, George wound up staying in The Spa City, marrying, and raising a family – eventually assuming the helm of his father's small, but thriving, insurance company that became known as Pierce, Pratt & Brown. (The business was sold to Matthew Gormley in 1984, but George continued to work there until around 1990.)

Although George never made it to the New York stage, son David Hyde Pierce insists his beloved father "was a performer all his life"—as a magician and an actor with the Town Hall Players, on the ski slopes, on the tennis courts, and, perhaps most memorably, on the dance floor.

His tireless efforts on behalf of Rotary began with his induction into the local club in 1938 and culminated with his being honored as a Paul Harris Fellow in 1996.

During that same half century, George Hyde Pierce also served the local community with devotion on behalf of the Bethesda Episcopal Church, the Boy Scouts, Greenwich Cemetery, and the Saratoga Hospital.

"He was an absolutely wonderful man, an inspiration, and a real sparkplug," recalls longtime Saratoga Rotarian, Hal Gerow. "George had a way of making everyone feel at ease. It didn't matter if you were a newcomer or if he'd known you for years, you just felt George was someone you could talk to and trust. He was polite and genteel, yet also extremely outgoing. If there was fun to be had, you could be sure George was one of the instigators or in the middle of it. He was a real mover and shaker without ever being rambunctious."

Only on the dance floor did the father of actor David Hyde Pierce let fellow Rotarians catch a glimpse of his show biz side. "We affectionately called him Twinkle Toes," laughs Gerow, "because he was a great dancer and you couldn't get him to sit down once the music started playing. He was dynamic! His wife Laura was wonderful, too. You just enjoyed being around them, because they were so positive and friendly."

Gerow also credits George with energizing Rotary Club meetings, fund-raisers, and community outreach projects.

"You could always count on George to volunteer. No matter how busy he was, he somehow found time to go where he was needed and do what needed doing with enthusiasm. For instance, he was one of the pioneers of the home show. I can't tell you how many hours he spent standing on the floor of the Old Armory welcoming visitors. That's a huge annual event in the city now, but it started with just a few dedicated individuals—George being among those who was especially generous with his time."

No wonder his son David cherishes so highly the honor bestowed upon him at the 75th anniversary of the founding of the Rotary Club of Saratoga Springs in 1999. By all accounts, there wasn't a dry eye in the room as David gave an emotional acceptance speech acknowledging the special Paul Harris Fellow awarded in recognition of his own shining example of a wonderful life that places "Service Above Self."

David told Saratoga Rotarians that of all the awards he had received, the Paul Harris Fellow was most dear to his heart "because it is the only one I share with my father."

At press time, David Hyde Pierce was winning rave reviews for performances on Broadway! To learn more about Rotary, please turn to page 142.

More than just a few minutes with Andy Rooney

Inasmuch as Andy Rooney had been a fixture in my parents' living room on Sunday evenings seemingly from the beginning of time, I was more than a little nervous when I finally summoned the courage to ask the "60 Minutes" regular for an interview. Imagine my surprise when this American icon answered his own telephone inside the CBS office he occupies in New York City!

Although I tried hard not to sound intimidated, I'm sure I hadn't spent more than a few minutes on the line with Andy Rooney before I managed to put one of my two left feet in my mouth. I'm equally certain he thought twice before taking any more early morning calls that hadn't been pre-screened by his secretary.

No wonder I almost needed smelling salts when a letter from the one and only Andrew A. Rooney arrived with a paragraph that read: "Your piece for the Summer 2003 edition of Saratoga Living *is exceptionally well done. I've been writing long enough to know how hard it is to get it right, and you did a job that amazes me. You not only got it right, you wrote it well. I am impressed."*

This would have been enough praise to keep my head in the clouds till my 90th birthday when I received an invitation from The Rooney Family to join them at a 90th birthday celebration for the commentator's fascinating older sister, Nancy Reynolds Rooney, with whom I bonded while working on the 2003 feature . . . and with whom I have since enjoyed many a lively conversation. (I'm still trying to figure out why Nancy never got her own talk show, but that's another story!)

BOTTOM LINE: Meeting Andy Rooney in person for the first time was one of the greatest thrills of my life. Being invited to sit directly across from him at a table was an honor I never expected. When he agreed to be photographed with me, I was struck dumb to such a degree that I failed to ask the person to whom I handed my camera if he had any idea how to take a picture. Suffice to say, I now have two keepsake photos of Andy Rooney grinning from ear-to-ear with his arm around -- a thumbprint! Hmmmmm. I see my favorite person named Andy (second only to my youngest brother, Andy) will be celebrating a 90th birthday of his own a few years from now. Would it be too crass for Little Annie Looney to crash the party and ask for a few minutes in one of those foolproof photo booths with Andy Rooney?

The following is an excerpt from the feature about Andy Rooney and his family which spanned 20 pages (including Then & Now photos) inside the Summer 2003 edition of the magazine.

The wit and wisdom of Andy Rooney have earned him legions of fans across the nation and around the world. As the author of several bestselling books, an award-winning syndicated newspaper column and a popular spot on CBS TV's *60 Minutes*, his face and voice rank among the most familiar of our times. Lesser known — but equally fascinating — is the part of Rooney's life that included more than a few minutes of boyhood adventures in the greater Saratoga/Capital Region.

For example, he doubts there's anyone alive who knew the barn behind 23 Church Avenue in Ballston Spa as well as young Andy Rooney. The Church Avenue house and barn originally belonged to his paternal grandparents (Charles P. Rooney of England and Annie Aitken Rooney of Portobello, Scotland) who acquired the property in 1905 when Rooney's father, Walter Scott Rooney, was in his late teens. Walter and his two older brothers, Fred and Bill, had spent their earlier years in residences on Ballston Avenue and Malta Avenue.

By the time Andrew Aitken Rooney came along on January 14, 1919, the property had become the matrimonial home of his beloved Uncle Bill and Auntie Belle. The couple initially moved in to help care for Rooney's widowed paternal grandmother and stayed there until their own deaths in 1950. Although Uncle Bill was better known throughout the area as William C. Rooney, a highly respected and community-minded attorney-at-law and Auntie Belle (nee Annabel Cole) earned accolades as a civic volunteer, their nephew admired and respected them for other reasons.

"Uncle Bill was the best friend a young boy could ever have," Rooney told *Saratoga Living* during a telephone interview. "I never lived in Ballston Spa . . . my parents moved to Albany before I was born . . . but we frequently came up from Albany -- and always spent Thanksgiving there. Dad's mother was still alive when I was very young and we'd come to see her and other relatives and friends who lived in the village."

"The first thing Uncle Bill did when we came was take me up Church Avenue to see his friend, Frank Winney. Frank had a butternut tree in his backyard and, if it was the season when the nuts were on the ground, we gathered them up and took them home. They were good in cookies, but the meat was difficult to extract from the shells."

113

Frank Winney ran the dry goods store on Front Street between Joe Sweeney's drug store and Uncle Bill's upstairs law office at 22 Front Street. While the late merchant's name can still be read in the tiles outside his once thriving store, no markers were left by Uncle Bill who later moved his practice to a building on Low Street near Wiswall Park.

"When we came to visit on Saturdays, Uncle Bill would take me by the hand and walk me along Front Street introducing me to the store owners. He knew them all by name and they all made me feel welcome." Best of all, though, were the times young Andrew shared with Uncle Bill at 23 Church Avenue. "I think he missed having children of his own and he enjoyed doting on us," reflects Rooney, with reference to himself and his older sister Nancy. "I must have explored the house and the barn from top to bottom 100 times with Uncle Bill between the ages of seven and 14."

Adding to the excitement was the fact that Rooney's late cousin Bob, who was 15 years his senior, had electrified the barn one summer while he was a student at RPI. Bob and his brother Charles lived with their father, Fred Rooney and his wife, Ella (nee Clements), on nearby McMaster Street.)

Although the horse and buggy had gone the way of the dinosaur by the 1930s, Rooney insists the barn still smelled like horses when he entered. And despite the fact that the historic structure was big enough for two cars, Uncle Bill never put his Reo inside "because the barn was filled with other treasures more valuable."

Earlier this year, Rooney recalled those treasures as including such artifacts as "old tools and an old horse saddle with various leather pieces." Old steamer trunks of part wood, part leather and clothing of bygone eras provided endless hours of discovery and play in the barn's attic.

"Uncle Bill never threw anything out," mused Rooney, a self-proclaimed "world class saver" of all manner of things sentimental and nostalgic as well as of things that might come in handy and/or come back into style one day.

Auntie Belle, meanwhile, had what Rooney dubbed "all the traditional virtues of a grand aunt. She was very loving and always had huge amounts of food prepared for us which we used to call the groaning board because it was always bad. Auntie Belle was a wonderful human being, but a lousy cook."

(FUN FOOTNOTE: What was Frank Winney's backyard is right next door to where the author's family has resided since 1968.)

114

In those days, Rooney recalls, "There were gardens all around the house with squash and pumpkins that my aunt later kept in storage with other farm fresh produce in a cool part of the basement."

The saddest day for his beloved aunt and uncle was the day the Haight House, once a palatial mansion complete with expansive servants quarters and outdoor tennis courts at the corner of East High Street and Church Avenue, was sold. Half of the magnificent landmark (originally occupied by Theodore Haight of the American Hide & Leather Company) was dismantled to make room for a gas station right next door to Auntie Belle and Uncle Bill. The gas station is now a laundromat. The remaining half of the Haight House still stands on the south side of East High Street, close to where Church Avenue (Route 50) intersects with it.

Happier memories for Rooney include accompanying his mother down to the Old Iron Spring along Front Street to sample the village's popular mineral waters -- though he is quick to add that "the charm of its taste escaped my young palate . . . I hated it!" Although he occasionally stopped at the Old Iron Spring for nostalgic reasons when passing through the village later in life, Rooney is adamant that the taste of the mineral water did NOT improve with age.

Sampling the sulfur-like water is one of the few unpleasant memories Andy has of his mother, born Ellinor Reynolds in Albany in 1886. When she was a small girl, Ellinor's British-born parents, Annie (nee Colvin) and John William Reynolds, moved their family, which also included sons Charles, William and Ralph and another daughter, Anna -- to Ballston Spa.

"My mother was raised in a big brown and yellow house known as Deer Park on Ralph Street. Her family had moved out before I got there," explains Rooney. The Deer Park property -- now called Kelley Park-- was known for its beautiful orchards and the Jersey cows kept by the Reynolds family. Rooney's sister, Nancy, says the Reynolds also kept pigs which were nourished solely with corn grown on the premises and milk from the Jersey cows.

Originally owned by Harvey Chapman in the 1840s and later run as a farm by Merritt J. Esmond, the Ralph Street property was purchased by the Reynolds in 1900 from Charles and Cora Blittersdorff.

When a fire damaged the house on New Year's Day 1914, Grandfather Reynolds sold what remained of the structure to Frank S. Hathorn and his wife Helen. When the property was subsequently used by the Catholic Church, the house was converted to a nunnery.

In the 1960s, a barn on the former Reynolds family homestead (in which Nancy recalls having seen the year 1860 in the slate roof) was burned to the ground by vandals -- ironically while a village fire pumper was being stored inside!

With the Civil War era barn went a piece of history Andy and Nancy's mother liked to relate involving the year a circus came to Ballston Spa. According to Rooney, one of the circus ponies broke his leg and their mother's brother Charley brought the little horse home and put it up in a sling in that barn hoping to save the horse's life. Sadly, the pony perished.

Rooney insists his maternal grandfather was "the principal source of brains" on his mother's side of the family. Having made his way from Redruth in Cornwall, England, when he was just 16, John William Reynolds went on to establish a successful foundry in Ballston Spa.

Grandfather Reynolds also patented half a dozen inventions including a tool with a handle whose opposite end fitted into an indentation in one end of the round iron lids of a wood stove. The handle had little ears near the base that acted as a fulcrum. Several years ago, Rooney checked around Ballston Spa and was delighted to find there were still some manhole covers in place in the village which had been made in his grandfather's foundry. All were clearly imprinted with the name REYNOLDS.

Legend has it that Andrew and Nancy Rooney's grandmother's father came to America "after being run out of Scotland" for trying to start a union in a paper mill a ferry's ride away from Glasglow and that "Grandma Annie" didn't come to this country until two years later because she initially didn't want to leave her homeland.

Given this colorful family history, it's not surprising that the union between Ellinor Reynolds and Walter Scott Rooney would produce children and grandchildren of distinction!

On August 29, 1911 -- a year after Walter graduated from Williams College -- he exchanged wedding vows with Ellinor in an evening ceremony at her parents' home on Ralph Street in Ballston Spa. A newspaper account described the bride as "one of Ballston's most attractive . . . and popular . . . young ladies." The Rev. Arthur T. Young officiated at the ceremony which was witnessed by Walter's brother, Bill, and Ellinor's close friend, M. E. ("Bess") Kerley. According to the newspaper, Miss Cassie Galloghly of Albany "played the strains of the wedding march" as the bridal party -- including bridesmaids Bess Valentine and Lucy McCreedy -- descended the stairway.

In a moving tribute published in 1980 following Ellinor Reynolds Rooney's death following a prolonged illness in her 94th year, Rooney noted that his mother had won the girls' high jump championship in Ballston Spa 1902 and that, throughout her long life, she "did a million kindnesses" for her loved ones. "There were a lot of things she wasn't good at, but no one was ever better at being a mother," he wrote, noting that she had "unlimited love and forgiveness in her heart for those close to her. Neither my sister nor I ever did anything so wrong in her eyes that she couldn't explain it in terms of right. She assumed our goodness, and no amount of badness in either of us could change her mind. It made us better."

On the lighter side, Rooney added that his mother, who was educated by private tutors, earned a reputation "for driving her old Packard too fast and too close to the right-hand side of the road."

Less has been written about Rooney's father simply because, he says: "I didn't know him as well as I knew my mother. He traveled a lot. . . he was away three weeks out of four every month and only home one week a month."

Rooney chuckles that his mother "didn't let my father in on things my sister and I did that might upset him. For example, she didn't dare show him my report cards; she signed them and sent them back to school before he came home." He's quick to add that his father, while quite demanding in many ways, also had an excellent sense of humor and spent quality time with his young son when he was not away on business. "Dad played on the Ballston High football team when he was a teenager and my friends all thought he was wonderful because he could always seem to relate to what we kids were going through at various stages of life. My sense of humor definitely came from my father."

In a commencement address to the 1998 graduating class of The Albany Academy, Rooney stated: "I never come up the driveway out front or enter this building without being flooded with great memories. I spent eight of the best years of my life at the Academy, one in the annex on Elk Street, one in the original old Academy building and six great years here in this building (on Academy Road). I know you wouldn't think so looking at me, but I know every nook and cranny of this building as well as all of you in uniform do."

As part of the same speech, Rooney told the Academy's 185th graduating class that he often dreams about what he'd do if he had two lives to live and that he'd be mighty tempted to start over on the grounds of The Academy.

"I'd start all over as a freshman, and, I can promise you, I'd be a much better student the second time than I was the first. I'd be better because I'd know it was a once-in-a-lifetime opportunity."

One of the other things he said he'd do with a second life is go back to college. After graduating from The Albany Academy with the Class of 1938, Rooney attended Colgate University, but his studies were cut short at the end of his junior year in 1941 when he was drafted into the US Army.

While stationed at Fort Bragg in March of 1942, he wed Marguerite ("Margie") Howard -- whom he had met at Mrs. Munson's dancing class in Albany at age 13. The daughter of prominent Albany orthopedist William P. Howard, Margie graduated from Bryn Mawr College in Pennsylvania in 1941. Quips Rooney: "Margie always likes to point out that she's a year younger than I am, but was a year ahead of me in college."

In February 1943, he was one of six correspondents who flew with the Eighth Air Force on the first American bombing raid over Germany. Some of his earliest writing was published in a military periodical where his editor was "a stickler" for accuracy.

Return to civilian life saw the Rooneys welcome four children -- Ellen, Martha, Emily and Brian -- while Rooney tackled assignments for popular CBS programs including "The Arthur Godfrey Show" (1949 - 55) and "The Garry Moore Show" (1959 - 65). From 1962 to 1968 he collaborated with the late TV correspondent Harry Reasoner (Rooney writing and producing; Reasoner narrating) on a number of CBS News Specials, including an award-winning script on Black America.

Somehow, he also managed to work in writing a twice-weekly column for Tribune Media Services. The column appears in 200 newspapers as well as a variety of magazines across the nation.

Although his 12th book, *Common Nonsense* had just hit book shelves and Internet stores when the interview for this story took place early in 2003, Rooney was already working on another full-length manuscript due out that fall. Titled *Years of Minutes*, the book features past 60 Minutes pieces drawn from his 25 years of commentaries on the highly rated Prime Time CBS News program. "I do 35 or 40 pieces for *60 Minutes* every year . . . it should be easy to fill a book," says the man once described by *TIME* magazine as "the most felicitous writer in television."

He is also among its most honored, having won the Writers Guild Award for Best Script of the Year six times -- more than any other writer in the history of the medium.

His unique commentaries also earned him Emmys in 1979, 1981 and 1982. On May 19, 2002, Rooney made headlines when he presented his 800th segment of *"A Few Minutes with Andy Rooney."*

Although proficient in computer usage, Rooney insists he still prefers to hammer out correspondence on the same old Underwood No. 5 typewriter that his Uncle Bill's trusty secretary Ethel Medbery had used to type his legal documents in Ballston Spa in the 1930s. Still an early riser, Rooney's alarm goes off promptly at 5:27 each morning. Why 5:27 rather than say, 5:30? "I hit the wrong button one day and never bothered to change it."

Over the decades, Rooney -- who resides in Connecticut -- has crafted many beautiful pieces of furniture and other functional and decorative objects in his woodworking shops at his vacation homes in Rensselaerville and Lake George. The Rensselearville woodwork shop measures 25' x 25' and is just 20 feet away from The Pentagon, a five-sided building (eight feet on a side) he built in 1988 so he would have a quiet place to write when vacationing with the family.

Although he contends he "can get tired of writing and be cutting wood in under a minute," the fact is that three of Rooney's books were written in the solitude of The Pentagon.

Because of surgery on his right arm to correct Carpel Tunnel Syndrome, Rooney hasn't been tackling many woodworking projects lately. "I don't think it's a good idea to get too close to a saw blade just yet," he laughs.

Having also had his leg injured last Christmas on his way to buy a newspaper in a blizzard, Rooney says he's content to be able to hold a raccquet and play tennis a few times a week. This summer, Rooney hopes to spend as much time as possible with Margie, their children and grandchildren and his sister, Nancy, at the tranquil camp on Lake George's Pilot Knob that has been in the family since 1926.

Those vacations will, no doubt, yield ideas for more than a few minutes of fresh television essays, newspaper columns and -- who knows? -- maybe even a bestselling book about some of the fascinating "faces behind the places" that captured a very young Andy Rooney's heart and mind right here in Saratoga County!

It is with sadness that I must note that Andy Rooney's beloved wife has since passed away. I consider myself privileged to have met Mrs. Rooney at the 90th birthday party she arranged for her sister-in-law in August of 2003. Marguerite Howard Rooney truly was "the hostess with the mostess."

Why so much ado
about Marylou?

When I think of Marylou Whitney, I think of a gracious hostess with a million dollar smile whose eyes twinkled merrily as she sipped ice tea with me during a private interview at her Cady Hill estate in Saratoga Springs.

I think of a woman who made my youngest daughter feel like a princess when our paths happened to cross in the lobby of the Saratoga Hospital a short time later. A volunteer was selling raffle tickets for the biggest Easter basket of bunny-shaped treats then little Kiersten had ever seen. In what can best be described as a spontaneous act of kindness, Marylou arranged for a longer than a rabbit's ear roll of raffle tickets to be placed in the tiny child's hands. When Kiersten asked me on the way to our car who "that nice lady" was. I responded: "Her name is Marylou Whitney . . . and I have a feeling that one day you'll be telling your own kids about the day you met her inside of the hospital where you were born."

A few months later -- after the story I wrote about Marylou appeared in print -- I felt like Cinderella when an invitation to The Whitney Gala arrived in my mailbox. Only a fairy godmother was missing as I prepared to depart for the event escorted by one of my best friends, Dave Sherwood.

One might think the flowing evening gown I was wearing would have made me completely forget my true identity as a journalist. Instead the celebrities who turned out for the affair brought out the old newspaper reporter in me! Before long, I found myself jotting down notes as I chatted with "I Dream of Jeannie" star Barbara Eden and "Dream Come True Comedy Queen" Joan Rivers. As gracious as she was dazzling, Barbara said it warmed her heart that a new generation had discovered Jeannie through the magic of reruns. When I found myself standing in a dessert line next to Joan, she was quick to heap compliments on the caterers and decorators as well as a local hairstylist who had fussed with her tresses.

Over the next few years, I had the joy of connecting with Marylou as she literally wore a broad variety of hats in at least as many different settings -- from festive functions at the Saratoga Race Course to elegant cocktail parties at the National Museum of Dance to a western BBQ to benefit the Double "H" Hole in the Woods Ranch in the foothills of the Adirondacks.

The image that brings the broadest grin to my face, however, is that of a picture Marylou granted me permission to publish with the first story I wrote about her in which she is sporting a fake tatoo to enhance her appearance as a "Motorcycle Mama" in a local parade.

The photo serves as a vivid reminder that there isn't much Marylou won't do to help a worthy cause. It also speaks volumes about why there's so much ado about Marylou . . . as (I hope) does this excerpt from the feature I wrote for the Summer 2000 edition of the magazine.

~~~

Widely credited with restoring a touch of class to the historic city that is home turf to The Sport of Kings and The Queen of Spas is Marylou Whitney. But there is far more to the celebrated socialite than meets the eye.

Behind the glamour and glitz that have elevated her to a status approaching royalty is a gem of a human being who has not allowed money or privilege to blind her to the things that ultimately matter most in life: family, friends -- and faith.

~~~

Within the walls of the magnificent mansion on the historic Saratoga County estate known as Cady Hill are many splendidly decorated rooms in which Marylou Whitney may find seclusion.

Yet when it is genuine serenity she seeks, the jet-setting socialite takes a short stroll to a simple white building on the pristine grounds that were once the site of a bustling stage coach stop.

"This is the place I come to for reflection and renewal . . . and to give thanks for my blessings," Marylou explains as she opens the doors to reveal a tiny chapel with an interior so humble, yet at the same time so peaceful and inviting, that one momentarily forgets the world outside.

With floors made of rustic boards from an old barn and pews crafted by Shakers of a bygone era, one's eyes can't help but focus on the most colorful object in the room: a statue of Christ from ancient Peru that rests upon an altar cloth hand-woven in muted earth tones from St. Augustine, Florida.

Marylou cannot count the times she has visited this sanctuary since she and her late husband Cornelius Vanderbilt ("Sonny") Whitney had it built decades ago to resemble an 1810 Dutch-style house to which they had taken a fancy.

"When your schedule requires that you must travel as much as I do, it is not always possible to attend regular church services, and so there is a chapel on each of the Whitney properties where I can go whenever I feel the need, day or night," she explains. "The chapel near our Kentucky home is also quite special. Sonny had it built using logs taken from a cabin that was owned by Daniel Boone's family around 1794."

Yet another chapel, this one constructed using twigs fashioned by early American craftsmen, is found in the Adirondacks. "It's quite a steep climb to get there, but it's well worth it," smiles Marylou, noting that representatives of four denominations endured the uphill trek for its consecration ceremony. Sometimes Marylou invites family, friends, and visiting dignitaries to join her for services in her private chapels. "Our chapel services tend to be rather simple and very touching. There's so much love, so much faith, and so many prayers, silent as well as spoken, that people can at times get emotional."

Once, she recalls, then Secretary of State Henry Kissinger, though not of the Christian faith, was moved to tears by a prayer service at the Kentucky chapel. Another time, those attending a service in the Adirondacks joined hands to pray for a bedridden, terminally-ill gentleman with the result that "you could almost feel electricity in the air." Three days later, beams Marylou, he was up and walking!

"To me, lighting candles in the chapel and saying special prayers is much more meaningful than sending flowers," she reflects.

It is a source of great joy to her that John Hendrickson, a successful businessman credited with having a great sense of humor and enormous strength of character, whom she wed in Alaska in 1997, shares her love of the Bible. "People who don't know us may find it surprising, but our faith is very important to us," says Marylou, an Episcopalian. "I cannot believe how very fortunate I am that I have known the love of two such wonderful men, one much older, and now one much younger, than I."

Seated once again at a table in a cheery pink and white sun room inside the 15-room Cady Hill manor house, one cannot help but wonder what it must be like to reside at this luxurious estate that is well-hidden from public view by high shrubbery and fences along Geyser Road.

It is, after all, almost impossible to spend a summer in Saratoga Springs without catching a glimpse of Marylou Whitney in the newspapers or on television. By far the most photographed personality of the racing season, the glamorous socialite is expected to have a smile on her face whenever she ventures out in public. Rarely does she disappoint those who have focused their lenses upon her.

What those images have failed to capture is something all the money in the world cannot buy: Marylou Whitney's radiance. The mere fact that there's been so much ado about Marylou in the national as well as the local press makes many people feel they know everything about this particular member of the Whitney dynasty. I certainly had my own set of preconceived notions prior to our tête-à-tête, however, it became clear soon after our interview got underway that I was in the presence of an individual about whom I, in fact, knew absolutely nothing.

What, I wondered, matters in life to Marylou Whitney?

Among the first topics the woman who has visited all seven continents addressed with earnestness was her concern for the level of patriotism in our nation. "I love this country so much and am proud to be an American. I have great respect for those in our military and can't bear to hear anyone say anything against America. Do young people today realize how fortunate they are to live in this great land of ours—to enjoy the freedoms that we have?" she wondered aloud.

A source of pride in the former actress's own life is that she had regularly entertained American troops through the USO (a role that requires "courage, a good back, and faith in God") since World War II. As hard as it is to reconcile Marylou Whitney's youthful appearance with that period in history of half a century ago, it is true! Indeed, she performed in Hollywood movies like "Missouri Traveler" (with Lee Marvin) prior to marrying and raising five children with C.V. Whitney.

(Marylou was a single mother who was selling real estate and acting in movies to support her four then young children – Hobbs, Henry, Marion Llewellyn, and Heather when she met Sonny Whitney in Arizona in 1957. The couple married in Nevada in January of 1958 and welcomed a daughter, Cornelia, a year-and-a-half later.)

Another concern she was quick to voice had to do with the amount -- and quality -- of time today's parents and children spend together.

"I hear of households where family members simply heat-up different dishes from the freezer in the microwave and go their separate ways at mealtime. When do they gather to talk about the day?" she asked, stressing her view that the evening meal is a tradition worth preserving.

During the four decades she and Sonny Whitney were wed, Marylou took enormous pride in cooking and homemaking – a fact well-documented in a book by her late husband entitled *Live a Year with a Millionaire* (Maple Hill Press, 1981).

In the prologue, Mr. Whitney wrote the following tribute to his wife, whom he affectionately called Mary.

"First, she always dresses beautifully for whatever scenario we are in. Second, she decorates and finishes all of our homes in ways that please her and me. Third, she invites the guests, seats the tables, and provides the entertainment for all the parties we give. Many of these are to raise money for worthwhile charities. Fourth, and by no means least, she is a truly great cook, and has kept me in good physical and mental health."

The closer one looks at Marylou's own life, the clearer it becomes that a dilettante she is not! Often portrayed by the media as a "social butterfly" who flits from one gala to the next during summer months when the rich and famous flock to "The City of Health, History, and Horses," Marylou is, in fact, a dedicated and diligent behind-the-scenes worker.

Rather than simply making an appearance at the posh fund-raising events to which she lends her name as a patron or honorary chair, those in the know say Marylou is usually actively involved in planning, often right down to selecting the paper for the invitations. (And that's saying tons considering she is chair or honorary chair of more than a dozen major summer events!).

Members of her staff at Cady Hill speak of Marylou with open admiration as well as a loyalty they clearly feel she has earned over the years. Priority is given to hiring locals -- from caterers and florists to musicians and printers. "I try to do all that I can, both directly and indirectly, to patronize businesses in and around Saratoga Springs," says Marylou.

"There is a ripple effect every time we have a gala. A lady may decide she needs a new gown, or at least a new pair of panty hose and she may also go out and get her hair done especially for the occasion. A gentleman may realize it's time to get his tuxedo cleaned or to buy a new pair of socks and shoes.

"And, of course, the hotels fill right up when it's time for The Whitney Gala and Travers Day festivities. In these and many other ways, I like to think that everyone in the community benefits from the galas – not just the charities for which we are raising funds."

Lending her ideas, as well as her special touch of class, to these banquets and balls is what helps ensure they will be a success. It is widely agreed that without Marylou neither the turnouts nor the amounts raised for worthy area causes would be as high.

On the flip side, Marylou can quickly distance herself from an organization when she feels honesty, integrity, or human rights are being compromised or violated. In a gutsy move that made headlines around the world earlier this year, the socialite withdrew financial support from the Whitney Museum of American Art after discovering it was featuring a controversial exhibit by a non-American artist that portrayed NYC Mayor Rudy Giuliani as a Nazi.

"This piece essentially consisted of trash cans and does a horrible injustice to Jewish people," insists Marylou, adding: "I despise anything that incites hate."

What does she hope her most enduring legacy will be?

"I want very much to leave the world a better place in which to live."

~~~

Mary Ann Mobley:
From 90210 to 12020

As touched as I was by the spontaneous act of kindness I witnessed between Marylou Whitney and my youngest daughter just before Easter 2000, I was moved to tears of joy upon receipt of a hand-written letter from her two years later. The correspondence arrived after Marylou learned that my first-born had been hospitalized due to life threatening complications from a disease about which our family then knew nothing. Marylou, on the other hand, was close friends with a celebrity spokesperson for the National Crohn's & Colitis Foundation: Mary Ann Mobley.

Not long thereafter an endearing voice with a hint of a southern accent came through the phone lines linking the west and east coasts.

Communications between the glamorous star's residence in the 90210 zip code area and our 12020 address soon became routine as the former Miss America did everything in her power to empower my daughter to turn this negative into a positive. Insisting that she be called not just once or twice, but about a dozen times over a period of months, Mary Ann gave a complete stranger's child reason to hope she might lead a full, productive life in the future. Always patient, kind and in good humor, Mary Ann listened so intently that my then 20-year-old later wrote: "I sensed she genuinely understood -- and felt -- my pain." There is no doubt that the actress ultimately played a leading role in Tara's decision to pursue a degree in nutrition with the long-term goal of becoming a registered dietician.

More than once, Mary Ann's husband (actor Gary Collins) also took time to lend an encouraging word. When Tara and I finally embraced this stellar pair in person at the 2003 Whitney Gala, we rejoiced in the knowledge that while east is east and west is west, the twain can -- and do -- meet.

Sometimes it's under the most extraordinary of circumstances . . . as when miles of smiles bridged the gap between 90210 and 12020.

If the eyes are the mirror of the soul, gazing into those through which Mary Ann Mobley views the world provides a glimpse into the breathtaking beauty of an earthbound angel.

Blessed with physical attributes and talent that made her a natural for the title of Miss America in 1959 and romantic roles opposite Elvis Presley in the early 1960s, Mobley soon proved herself to be more than just another pretty face. Indeed, she has the distinction of being the only pageant winner ever to achieve wide success on the big screen as well as on Broadway and prime time TV upon completion of her reign as Miss America.

Her dedicated work as a humanitarian is legendary and she has earned a reputation as a tireless champion for a number of health-related organizations. The courage she demonstrated in breaking the silence about her own struggles with Crohn's Disease won the southern belle accolades as a true steel magnolia.

Mobley's most heart-wrenching and, occasionally dangerous, assignments have taken her to Cambodia, Ethiopia, Mozambique, Somalia, Kenya, Simbawe and the Sudan, where she filmed award-winning documentaries providing in-depth looks at the plight of millions of children who are helpless victims of war and deprivation.

It was a pioneering endeavor both because she was the lone female in a five-member crew and also because hers was the first American television production team to enter Communist Cambodia. Among the men in the entourage was her husband, award-winning actor/talk show host Gary Collins. It was during the time Collins was on location filming the television series *Born Free* that the couple had first witnessed the children's suffering first-hand.

With a beautiful home awaiting them upon their return home to their posh Beverly Hills 90210 address, the couple could easily have turned their backs on the misery half way around the world. Instead, they vowed to do something to educate global audiences about what they had observed so that similar tragedies might be prevented from happening in the future.

Together for the better part of four decades, Mobley and Collins consider themselves "best friends" and realize that they are a rare Hollywood twosome not just because of their marital bliss, but also because they've have had the same address and the same telephone number for as many years as they've been wed.

Mobley awards credit for the domestic stability to her better half. "Gary's a saint," she told *Saratoga Living* in 2003.

If not quite ready for canonization, Collins is certainly every bit as warm and personable as when he earned an Emmy while hosting the long-running *Hour Magazine* TV talk show in the 1980s. Recently honored with his own star on Hollywood's famous Walk of Fame, Collins is also active in the March of Dimes and relief organizations to end world hunger. In addition, he enthusiastically supports his wife's work on behalf of the National Crohn's and Colitis Foundation.

The couple, who enjoy visiting Saratoga Springs in the summer as guests of Marylou Whitney, met shortly after Mobley was initially diagnosed as having Crohn's in her 20s. "I had just won a Golden Globe and was feeling on top of the world. I really thought I had the world on a string . . . I had just finished a month on a movie called `Three On A Couch' with Jerry Lewis and Janet Leigh. It was a wonderful shoot, but a hard shoot, and when I came back to Los Angeles from location, I was not feeling well. I didn't have a doctor in LA, but found a nice physician who put me in the hospital where they ran all sorts of tests. After two weeks and all sorts of torturous things, the doctors came in and informed me that I had an incurable disease."

In fairness to the doctors, Mobley says even they didn't know much about Crohn's four decades ago except that symptoms typically included diarrhea (often watery and/or bloody), severe abdominal and/or intestinal pain and chills. Another word used to describe it was "debilitating."

To say Mobley was initially devastated would be an understatement. Then single and far from her family and friends in her Mississippi hometown, she vividly recalls feeling incredibly isolated and frightened.

Dehydrated and anemic from diarrhea and internal bleeding and limping like Festus from "Gunsmoke", the budding young actress was advised to abandon her show business aspirations because he felt the stress was triggering the attacks. That physician urged her to have surgery.

"But God must have been with me because I felt strongly that there had to be another answer. That answer turned out to be another doctor by the name of Martin Pops. He smiled at me, and said not to worry . . . that we would live with this with dignity and there would be no surgery unless there was no other alternative. I left his office feeling that no longer was I going to be a victim . . . I had a hand in my own battle."

"I subscribed to *Prevention Magazine* and read everything I could about nutrition and Crohn's Disease, and though I'm certainly not a doctor, I began my steps to remission through the use of conventional medicine and vitamin therapy."

128

With her improved health came guest spots on shows like *Fantasy Island* and recurring roles as Dr. Beth Everdeen on the TV drama *Falcon Crest* and as Maggie McKinney Drummond on the popular sitcom *Diff'rent Strokes*. Ironically, she never missed a day's filming. In addition to her stage, movie and TV work, the multi-talented Mobley also performed death defying trapeze acts in CBS "Circus of the Stars" shows -- not to mention scuba diving with sharks and flying with the Blue Angels in an F-18.

"There still isn't a cure for Crohn's, but there is much those of us with the disease can do to prevent the symptoms from worsening and to greatly improve the quality of our lives."

When the beautiful and glamorous movie star later made the courageous decision to break the silence about her own experiences with Crohn's Disease and ulcerative colitis, she offered an enormous ray of hope to the two million men, women and children who suffer from the disorder. Her affiliation with the National Crohn's and Colitis Foundation has drawn much needed attention to the cause and the need for more research and better treatment options.

Mobley has also done much to help raise awareness of -- and support for -- the March of Dimes, the Susan G. Komen Breast Cancer Foundation, the National Council on Disability, The Exceptional Children's Foundation for the Mentally Retarded and many other charitable organizations.

She is most proud of The Mary Ann Mobley Pediatric Wing at the Rankin General Hospital in her hometown of Brandon, Mississippi.

In retrospect, Mobley realizes she drew fortitude from the faith foundation that was cemented in her childhood by the local church community and by her mother, Mary Holmes, and maternal grandmother, Mary Stuart Farrish.

"I grew up in Brandon -- a small town of 2,500 where it was the norm for children to attend Sunday school at 10 a.m. followed by the main service at 11 a.m. In the evening, we'd return to the church for a youth fellowship meeting. On Wednesdays, we'd head back again for evening prayer meetings and choir practice," remembers Mobley, who donated the first $2,500 pay check she received for her work as a Miss America to buy a new bell for Brandon's Methodist Church.

For her, it was the most natural of gestures -- her way of giving something back to the community that had done so much to nurture and encourage her. "You have to understand that in Brandon, I didn't belong just to my family. I belonged to the town. Everyone looked out for one another's children. There was a real feeling of belonging."

Mobley credits her mother's mother -- who went by the nickname "Manie" and lived to be 101 -- with encouraging her both to dream and to stand up for her beliefs with conviction . . . albeit in a ladylike fashion.

"When I would visit my grandmother as a little girl, I just loved to listen to her stories! At night we'd say our prayers together. As I was falling asleep, she'd tell me to wait under the big oak tree in Fairyland and tell her what I was wearing so she'd recognize me when she got there. I'd tell her I had on a white satin dress that sparkled because it was decorated with a handful of stars. I always had gardenias in my hair," Mobley fondly recalls. Her late grandmother was usually dressed in lavender chiffon, wearing a lavender leghorn hat and carrying a bouquet of violets.

Mobley says her grandmother would also read to her for hours. "Studies that were done after my grandmother's time have shown that children associate being held and being read to as comforting, nurturing experiences. And so, even though TV is a large part of my business, I believe that we (as a nation of parents) need to spend more time reading to our children."

It was something Mobley and Collins did when their daughter was growing up -- with positive results. Christened "Mary" in keeping with a family tradition that the first-born girl in each generation on the Farrish side of the family be given that first name and "Clancy" in honor of Mobley's paternal grandfather, William Clancy, the couple's only child is now Senior Vice-President of Development for MGM Television.

"I just did a job for her so we've come full circle. Now she's hiring me. Gary and I are really proud of her. We like her; we love her; we respect her," says Mobley.

That beautiful feeling is clearly mutual . . . not bad considering the fact that Dad has earned a star on the world-famous Hollywood Walk of Fame for his incredible acting abilities and an Emmy for his outstanding work as a TV talk show host. While Gary Collins is unquestionably one of America's most versatile and respected entertainers, the role in which he takes the greatest pride is that of husband, father and active volunteer in relief organizations to end poverty, disease and world hunger.

It was while in the service of his country that Collins began his acting career. Stationed with the US Army in Europe, the California native tackled an assignment as a radio and television personality for the Armed Forces Network. The highlight during his work in musicals and dramas abroad was a Best Actor Award for his performance in *The Rainmaker* at the Paris International Drama Festival in 1959.

Taking his discharge in Europe, Collins made his film debut in *Cleopatra* starring the legendary Elizabeth Taylor and Richard Burton. Next came *The Pigeon That Took Rome* . . . then it was on to Paris for *The Longest Day*. He subsequently toured the Netherlands in a musical revue for KLM Airlines, appropriately titled *Say Cheese*.

Returning to the USA, Collins was cast in the Broadway production of Tennessee Williams' *The Train Doesn't Stop Here Anymore."* This was followed by a summer at the world famous Barter Theater in Abingdon, Virginia, before he headed to Greece for *Stranded* which became an entry in the 1963 Cannes Film Festival.

Christmas of 1964 found Collins back in Los Angeles where he acted in a string of TV series. These included *The Iron Horse, The Sixth Sense* and *Born Free* which was filmed entirely on location in Kenya in 1973. Collins continued his movie career throughout this period with appearances in the original *Airport, Houston, We've Got A Problem* and *Hangar 18*. Among his most recent film work was *Beautiful*, directed by Sally Field and co-starring Minnie Driver.

In addition, Collins has given stellar performances in many other made-for-TV movies including *Roots* -- the most watched mini-series in history.His easygoing style, warmth and concern earned Collins both an Emmy Award and his own star on Hollywood's famous Walk of Fame. More recent TV appearances on *Friends and Dharma & Greg* proved the seasoned actor's comic timing is as sharp as ever.

For all his accomplishments on stage and screen, Collins is perhaps almost as well known for his years as the host of Westinghouse's long-running *Hour Magazine* and ABC's *The Home Show.*

Collins also found time in between other career engagements to host the Miss America Pageant for nine years. Wed to former Miss America and actress Mary Ann Mobley, the versatile performer finds time to sing in summer musicals with his wife and both are in constant demand as speakers.

Both Collins and Mobley are active volunteers for numerous causes and charities, most notably the March of Dimes, the Crohn's and Colitis Foundation, the Susan G. Komen Foundation for Breast Cancer Research and several organizations that address global hunger, such as World Vision.

They are, without a doubt, two of the TRULY "Beautiful People."

No wonder faces light up when these stars come out . . . day or night.

Each is a class act as well as an act that is hard -- but very much worth the effort of trying -- to follow!

Maestro Charles Dutoit
& The Magic Baton

A child once asked if the baton raised by Maestro Charles Dutoit at the start of a concert was a magic wand. A silly question? Not to anyone who has ever fallen under the spell of the master conductor as he leads mesmerizing performances by The Philadelphia Orchestra at the Saratoga Performing Arts Center (SPAC) each summer.

According to Dutoit, the sounds that so enchant symphony audiences are the result of incredibly talented musicians who work incredibly hard at perfecting their talents for each and every program. While not quite a musical boot camp, the orchestra's August residency at SPAC is no vacation either!

"Summers in Saratoga are exciting, of course, but also very hard work for myself and the orchestra because we do something like 12 programs in just 17 days. We don't just jump up on the stage and improvise; there is a lot of preparation. We must all get up early to rehearse after the previous evening's performance. It is very concentrated," Dutoit explained during a telephone interview from the faraway hotel where he was staying.

Despite being on the road much of the year, the renowned conductor never missed a beat when it came to answering questions -- and actually kept me on my toes with his witty responses. This maestro is to be applauded as a gentleman of exceptional charm and grace. Seeing him in action at SPAC -- as I have been fortunate enough to do several times over the years -- is always an uplifting experience.

What follows are notes from a piece I wrote for Saratoga Living as Monsieur Dutoit was preparing to return to SPAC as Principal Conductor and Artistic Director for the 16th time in 2005.

If it were possible to give a standing ovation using nothing but words, Maestro Charles Dutoit has just awarded one to The Philadelphia Orchestra with whom he is celebrating his 25th year as conductor.

"Conducting this orchestra is like playing your own instrument and the other way around, too," mused Dutoit. "We know each other so well now that if I were an instrument, they (the musicians) could play me. We've been together so long, we are like one big family. It would not be possible to accomplish this with any other orchestra."

Dutoit, who also conducted in Europe and Asia during the year marking the milestone, expressed delight that some of the world's best soloists would be joining his orchestra as part of SPAC's 40th anniversary celebrations. Among the acclaimed artists who shared the spotlight during the season were cellist Yo-Yo Ma, violinist Itzhak Perlman and pianist Andre Watts.

Calling the audiences who patronize SPAC "absolutely wonderful" (the maestro loves to see families spread out blankets on the lawn where little children can romp while gaining early exposure to the classics!), Dutoit insisted that the only downside to performing inside the Saratoga Springs ampitheatre is the weather.

"The most difficult part is to cope with the heat and humidity. At times, the humidity is killing ... it actually makes it hard to breathe sometimes. This can be difficult and taxing for the musicians," explains Dutoit.

It can also be frustrating when severe thunderstorms arise. "We work so hard and want the weather to cooperate, but Saratoga weather changes so quickly. What are you going to do? You cannot fight with God."

On a happier note, Dutoit was looking forward to unwinding after performances by enjoying late meals at local restaurants. Among his favorite places to dine is Chez Sophie -- which recently moved from its longtime location in Malta to The Saratoga Hotel on North Broadway.

"I started going there when Sophie was still alive, and the Parkers (Paul, Cheryl and Joseph) are good, old friends. I go there often to enjoy the company as well as the food," Dutoit said.

(It should be noted that the Swiss-born conductor enjoys other styles of cooking as well. If you spot someone who looks like the conductor at the table next to yours in a different fine dining establishment, it most likely is the maestro himself!)

Breakfast, on the other hand, is usually prepared by Dutoit in the kitchen of a house he rents near Saratoga Lake. Staying there, rather than at a hotel, makes it possible to enjoy a home-away-from-home ambiance.

Best of all, Dutoit's daughter Annie (who teaches at Columbia University) and the conductor's two-year-old grandchild were planning to join him there for part of the summer. He hoped to enjoy many walks and shopping excursions with his loved ones in between rehearsals and performances.

The maestro insists, however, that the best souvenirs of Saratoga cannot be bought in any store. "Over the years, I have gathered many beautiful souvenirs ... fond memories of people I have met in the community and at the performing arts center. Of course, each concert is also a treasure. Each is special to me for a different reason."

When told that many people sing his praises -- not just as a conductor extraordinaire who has brought some of the most innovative and exciting programming ever to SPAC audiences -- but also as a genuinely gracious and thoughtful human being, Dutoit responded with trademark humility.

"It is true that I do enjoy saying hello to the people who work behind-the-scenes at SPAC ... I don't know everyone yet, but I try to go to the office two or three times each year. It's very nice to know who they are. It's just one way to let them know their contribution (to the arts) is important and appreciated. We could possibly not accomplish all that we do without them."

What did Maestro Dutoit plan to do after taking his final bow of the 2005 season at SPAC? Suffice to say his baton didn't have a chance to gather any dust!

So much does Dutoit travel that he maintains apartments in Buenos Aries, Montreal, Paris and Toyko as well as owning a country home in his native Switzerland. The fact that he speaks several languages makes it easy for him to live life to the fullest while on the road.

He sometimes even finds opportunities to improvise!

Meet the folks at Peckhaven Publishing

Laughing till the cows
come home is a
specialty of the house!

How a hunt and peck typist's
hunt for a book publisher led
to a couple of Pecks . . . and
lots of udder stuff that's sure
to grow on you if you'll JEST
give the seeds time to sprout!

I've been known to hunt and peck for letters of the alphabet on a keyboard, but never dreamed that my hunt for a book publisher would lead me to a Peck! Oh, what the hay! I literally lucked into a couple of Pecks: Joe and Pat, the perky proprietors of Peckhaven Publishing as well as historic Peckhaven Farm in Saratoga Springs, New York.. Funnily enough, I wasn't looking for a publisher for this book when I contacted the Pecks in the Spring of 2006. My intention was to harvest advice on where to get a local history book published later this year. Yet somehow between cups of coffee at a Friendly's, the conversation turned to possibilities for updating and expanding the manuscript I'd started several years earlier with a cast of characters that included productive barnyard critters such as egg-laying chickens and destructive intruders like porcupines and skunks. Before the creamer on our table was empty, we'd decided it would be udder nonsense not to pool our resources on this project -- especially since I'd once had the pleasure of writing an article about Joe and a book he wrote titled: "A Cow in the Pool & Udder Humorous Farm Stories" I hope reprinting that story here will better acquaint you with my publishers -- who, by the way, will also be handling my next book (Ballston Spa: The Way We Were; The Way We Are) -- which is due to roll off the presses early in 2007.

Saratoga County author Joe Peck doesn't mind if people say he's milking his life as a dairy farmer for all it's worth -- just as long as they laugh until the cows come home when they turn the pages of his book.

Aptly titled *A Cow in the Pool & Udder Humorous Farm Stories*, Peck's knee-slapping 230-page collection of musings draws upon his experiences at Peckhaven Farm. Except for his post-secondary years at Cornell University, Peck has always lived on the historic family farm which is set on a rise halfway between Saratoga Springs and Schuylerville with dazzling views of Vermont.

It is here that his 100 registered Holstein cows (one of whom really did fall into the Peck's swimming pool!) yield more than two million pounds of milk a year and where 100 acres of corn and 130 of alfalfa are grown and harvested annually. With so much growing and flowing going on around the old Peck homestead, one can't help but wonder how the dawn-to-dusk farmer ever found the time to take on the added responsibilities of self-publishing and promoting a book.

Since his first book -- featuring drawings and caricatures by Ballston Spa native Andrew R. Taormina -- rolled off of the presses a few years ago, Peck has not only gotten the cows milked on time, he's also attended book signings in settings ranging from libraries to feed stores and enlivened speaking engagements on behalf of the National Speakers Association and Toastmasters.

In addition, for several years Peck wrote a humor column for a number of rural publications including *American Agriculturalist* magazine, which reached 35,000 farmers monthly. He's also penned more than 150 columns, written free of charge for Cornell Cooperative Extension's agricultural news magazine that circulates in several Capital Region counties.

It's NOT udder nonsense to note that Peck's book was a family affair. His wife, Pat, a retired nutrition educator for Cornell Cooperative Extension, plowed through the word processing maze while daughter Sharon, a professor of reading at SUNY Geneseo, helped weed through and organize the stories into chapters. Son and business partner David tackled extra chores on the farm while his father wrote. Son-in-law Sean Kelleher (wed to Peck's other daughter, Toastmaster Debbie Peck Kelleher) designed and maintains the author's colorful web site. In addition, the entire Peck family has also been recognized by the Governor of New York for their contributions to agriculture and their community.

"It helps to have a sense of humor to work on a farm," muses Peck. "We're busy. Everything has to be done on time, all the time. The cows have to be milked twice a day. You don't leave them waiting."

Unfortunately, he observes, people are often so busy, they don't take time to see the lighter side of farm life -- such as the heifer falling in the pool in the middle of winter. An example from the pages of Peck's book explain how this was especially funny to a neighbor, who watched it happen from her kitchen window.

"There's a cow in the pool!'" she shouted. "Now, that's what I call bad news,'" he replied. Should he dial 911, call a vet or try CPR? The cow came out unhurt after being hoisted by a tractor. She was exceptionally clean and white, Peck observed. After the incident the family put a fence around the pool and keeps the gates locked.

The author is proud of the fact that Peckhaven Farm dates back to when the first Pecks settled in Saratoga County in 1803. Originally owned by Henry and John Wagman whose sister married Amos Peck, the farm originally had other crops and barnyard critters.

But since the only way for a modern farming operation to survive is to specialize, Peck chose cows whom he describes as "big animals -- not necessarily stupid -- but not awfully bright. Creatures of habit . . . as long as you do things at the same time everyday, they'll go along."

Sometimes, however, they don't understand what the farmer wants them to do and it's then Peck says, it's "easy to lose your temper but more fun to see the funny side."

~~~

Since the preceding magazine article was published in 2004, Peckhaven Publishing has published a second book by Joe Peck titled *A Tractor In The House & Other Smashing Farm Stories*. Readers of this newest volume will experience the frustrations of getting stuck in the mud, dealing with smart cows and computers, and having a tractor smash into the house. From recycled barns and electricity to hilarious descriptions of characters found at farm auctions, Joe's keen observations of the lighter side of farming will entertain and inspire readers from all walks of life.

FOR MORE INFORMATION, PLEASE CONTACT

Peckhaven Publishing
Peckhaven Farm
178 Wagman's Ridge Road
Saratoga Springs, NY 12866

518.584.4129

joe@joepeckonline.com
www.joepeckonline.com

A publishing Post Script from the author

Although Pat Peck's editing roots run deep, it's only been in recent years that the fruits of her labors have been shared with readers outside of select academic and Cornell Cooperative Extension circles.

A graduate of Bethlehem Central High School in Delmar, Pat received a B.S. in Nutrition and Education from Cornell University, College of Home Economics (now Human Ecology); and an M.S. in Education from the College of St. Rose before wedding Joe whom she'd met at Cornell,

Pat subsequently taught home economics at Shenendehowa Central for two years before starting a family. For the better portion of the next 17 years, Pat was mostly a stay-at-home mom, though she did put in occasional hours with the 4-H program at Cornell Cooperative Extension -- a commitment which increased with the retirements of Mildred Solberg and Al Lounsbury, two of the state's most outstanding 4-H agents.

When there was an opening for a full-time 4-H home economist in 1984, Pat asked the Peck kids if they thought they could manage if she were to work full-time and they said, "Go for it!" (Sharon, the couple's youngest was nearly 14 at the time while Debbie was 17 and David was a college sophomore.)

"Somehow my editing skills became known as I was asked to edit a lot of material and newsletters in the 4-H area and later in the home economics and even agricultural areas. I also volunteered to review both daughters' Masters theses, and Sharon's PhD dissertation, as well as Joe's monthly columns for the Ag News, so I have been editing -- at least for spelling, grammar, and logic and flow for quite some time. And then there were Joe's two books -- lots of opportunity for eye strain!" she quips.

Speaking of which . . . should you spot any typos or other errors inside of this book, it's not because Pat or other members of our editing team missed them.

Having suffered a retinal tear a couple of weeks prior to publication, I actually contemplated changing the title of this book to something along the lines of : *The Blurry Lines Behind the Bylines*. All kidding aside, the diminished vision in my left eye made it challenging to complete the final edits on my computer. Please try to overlook any oversights. We all did our best to "humor our stress" and, if you found yourself smiling as you read this labor of love, then I'll be the happiest one-eyed hunt and peck typist on the continent.

What can I say, but the AYES have it that Pat's career as a book publisher is sure to continue blossoming for years to come! As far as I can see, Pat's no longer a budding editor, but one in full bloom. Rarely have I encountered someone as adept as weeding out manuscript errors while maintaining a sunny disposition. I sincerely hope Pat will make room in her publishing garden for more of my own story ideas to sprout!

EGG-stra special thanks

I've never been one to count my chickens before they hatch, but I do believe in counting my blessings each and every day. I also believe in giving credit where it's due . . . and, in some cases, where it's L-O-N-G overdue. With that sentiment in mind, I would like to acknowledge the contributions of the following individuals who helped to make this book a reality.

In order of appearance in my writing life, I would like to thank the following: Steve Toussaint, who encouraged me to read between the lines and pen essays from the heart at Ballston Spa High School; T. J. Allen, Ben Rose and Jake Fennell, who drilled the 5Ws (and HOW!) into my head and showed me how to get most of the red out of the assignments I turned in prior to my graduation from the Journalism Program at Sheridan College in Oakville, Ontario; Jim Dills and Roy Downs, who picked me up when I faltered while taking my first baby steps as a full-time reporter-photographer at *The Canadian Champion* in Milton, Ontario; Phil Bingley, David Kingsmill and Michael Shapcott, who let me take a break from my otherwise serious duties as a police and court reporter to show off my funny side in the special April Fool's Editions published by the *Oakville Journal Record*; Norm Alexander, Robert Ashe, Wilma Blockhuis, Rod Jerred, Barb Joy, Howard Mozel, John Robinson, Carol Stewart-Kirkby, Kathy Yankus, and other staffers (including editorial cartoonist Steve Nease) who collectively made my news editing stint at *The Oakville Beaver* the most rewarding of my entire career; the ROS staff at the Ontario Ministry of Agricultural & Food in Guelph, Ontario, who taught me about the "ruralities" of writing for farm publications; Fran Fearnley and Holly Bennett, who allowed me to inject humor into many feature articles I wrote for *Great Expectations* and *Today's Parent* when my first two kids were small.

Closer to home, a huge debt of gratitude is owed to my mother, Audrey Bopp Hauprich, and my brother, Francis G. Hauprich, for never missing a Red Pen Party in conjunction with *Saratoga Living* magazine from May of 1998 until it was sold in May of 2004 . . . and for humoring me through much of the editing process linked to this book; my partner, Cole Broderick, and my children, Tara, Marietje and Kiersten, for assisting with the re-typing of old stories and/or the re-scanning of old images I feared were lost forever after the PC I used in the 1990s fried to a crisp; my friend-to-the-end Wendy Hobday Haugh of Burnt Hills, NY, and her computer-savvy husband, Chuck Haugh, who deserve a "Rescuers Down Under" citation after cracking one high-tech mystery after the next, making it possible for me to open files that would otherwise still be floating around some place in Cyber Space; Donna & Pete Martin at The Village Photo and Mary Lewis at The Blue Caboose Framery in Ballston Spa -- who cheerfully assisted with recovery operations involving the cover artwork.

To all of the above: THANK YOU! And, yes, I am well aware that the preceding text included at least one run-on sentence that would be neigh-on-impossible to diagram without harming one's diaphragm. Not to worry, though. It only hurts when you DON'T laugh!

Skaal, Scandinavia!
A literary toast to Rotary

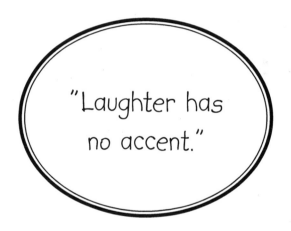

"Laughter has
no accent."

Why a portion of the proceeds
from the sale of this book
will be donated to Rotary-
sponsored literacy programs

SKAAL, Scandinavia!
A literary toast to Rotary

It doesn't happen every night. In fact it happens less often as time goes by, but sometimes I dream in Danish. And when I do, I'm inevitably whisked back to a magical summer 35 years ago when I landed in Copenhagen with two dozen Rotary International exchange students from across the USA and Canada.

Looking back, I can't help but ponder how fitting it was that my first two weeks in Scandinavia were spent in the charming city of Odense -- birthplace of Hans Christian Andersen, whose fairy tales had brought so much joy to my childhood as an *Ugly Duckling* of sorts in New York State.

As one who endured playground teasing after spinal meningitis left me looking anemic and anorexic -- complete with a swan-like neck -- I had not dared to fantasize about anything adventurous or glamorous in my future. I'd pretty much resigned myself to quietly studying art at a local college until the Hippie equivalent of a nearsighted Prince Charming came along on his noble steed and whisked me off to a castle in the clouds -- or at least a house in the suburbs with a white picket fence!

All of this changed when a perky young woman showed up at the high school in the quaint village where my family had recently been transplanted and began sharing her experiences as a Rotary International exchange student.

To say I was spellbound as I listened to Melissa speak about her year representing The Rotary Club of Ballston Spa in Holland would be an understatement. I remain eternally grateful to Missy and her Rotarian father, Dr. Jack Westbrook, for encouraging me to fill out an application for the program.

This was, without a doubt, the first phase of a Rotary-induced metamorphosis from an awkward adolescent to a seasoned journalist who would champion social-justice issues and talk her way into exclusive celebrity interviews.

From the moment I received a letter from Arlington Van Dyke (then Vice-Chairman of the Youth Exchange Program for District 7190) informing me that I would be hosted by The Rotary Club of Kolding, Denmark during the 1971 - 1972 academic year, I began to look at the world -- and my place in it -- from a refreshingly new perspective.

For the first time in my life, I dared to dream about what it might be like to cross an ocean and sink or swim on my own merits while totally immersed in a foreign language and culture on another continent. The prospect was at once exhilarating and daunting, but I wasted no time in securing a part-time job on weekends to save sufficient funds for my return passage.

Warmly welcomed by my first host family (who lived on a 300-year-old estate complete with a stork perched atop the thatched roof), I felt surprisingly at home. My residency with The Vistofts in the enchanting hamlet of Hjarup and later with The Gregersens and The Dreschers in Kolding yielded a treasure trove of memories -- as well as laying the groundwork for a lifetime of enrichment and service opportunities.

* * *

BECAUSE OF ROTARY . . . I got to explore parts of Denmark that were not ordinarily sought out by tourists -- such as an isolated dot on the map where a dialect on the brink of extinction was still spoken and to meet Danes in settings as humble as barnyards and as grand as castles where medieval battles had once been fought.

BECAUSE OF ROTARY . . . I was blessed with all-expenses-paid excursions to nearby countries including Sweden, Germany, Holland, Belgium and Switzerland. Most compelling for me were the house where Anne Frank penned her famous diary and the hallowed grounds which inspired the poem that begins: "In Flanders Field where poppies grow." It was during these sojourns that many a humanitarian seed was sown -- though some would take longer than others to blossom or be harvested.

BECAUSE OF ROTARY . . . I learned how to read, write and converse in a language I did not previously know existed. Suffice to say the experience made me empathetic to the plight of those I would later encounter who were struggling to master English as a Second Language as well as an advocate of literacy programs both at home and abroad.

BECAUSE OF ROTARY . . . I became familiar with the wit and wisdom of Danish philosopher Piet Hein whose adages have provided priceless motivation and inspiration. A favorite: *"He who lets the small things blind him leaves the great undone behind him."* Another who inspired me was Danish entertainer Victor Borge. His observation that *"A smile is the shortest distance between two people"* certainly proved to be true when I extended my hand with a Danish greeting at the start of interviews with NYC Ballet Master Peter Martins and the late Carl Holmen of Carlsberg Breweries. These truly GREAT Danes proved that *"Laughter has no accent."*

BECAUSE OF ROTARY . . . my parents and nine siblings welcomed a Brazilian lad named Marcio de Melo into our American-As-Apple-Pie home after I decided to return to Denmark to work as a governess for a school inspector's family. The following year, one of my brothers (College of St. Rose alum, Francis) accepted an invitation to reside with Marcio's family in South America and proved to be a formidable goodwill ambassador. In a new and exciting development, Marcio's daughter, Natalia, will be hosted by The Rotary Club of Ballston Spa during the 2006 - 2007 school year.

BECAUSE OF ROTARY . . . The web of friendship that includes the aforementioned Danish and Brazilian people also extends into Canada which was my home for a 15-year period starting in 1974. This adventure began after Ella Haley (who also spent 1971 - 1972 in Kolding . . . in her case representing the Rotary Club of Brantford, Ontario) urged me to check out colleges when I journeyed north of the border to visit her family. Now a professor, Ella and I remain kindred spirits. Whenever reunited, we giggle and come up with countless excuses to raise our glasses (now more likely to be filled with SNAPPLE than SNAPS) and proclaim: "Skaal!" While in Canada, I also had the joy of serving as an honorary Big Sister of sorts to Mette Ornstrup Christensen, a Rotary exchange student from Esbjerg, Denmark who was being hosted by The Rotary Club of Milton, Ontario. I also have fond memories of Danish-Canadian celebrations at Sunset Villa.

144

BECAUSE OF ROTARY . . . I became a writer. Ironically the hardest thing to get used to in all three homes that hosted me as an exchange student was having a bedroom all to myself -- something I'd not experienced during my first 18 years of life. The opportunity for nocturnal solitary confinement unleashed a creative side I might not otherwise have unearthed. Free to burn the midnight oil without causing a roommate to complain of sleep deprivation, I would spend hours writing in a journal and occasionally penning essays about the everyday life of an American teen in Denmark. Some of my "Words of Art" were published in my hometown newspaper and ultimately paved the way for my admission into the Journalism Program at Sheridan College in Oakville, Ontario. I subsequently had the honor of serving on the college's Journalism Advisory Committee and overseeing the conception and birth of a newspaper for its Brampton campus where the stork Steve Nease drew for my 1981 baby shower was a guest of sorts!

BECAUSE OF ROTARY . . . I BECAME A ROTARIAN! As a member of The Rotary Club of Ballston Spa, I am honored to be in the company of beautiful minds and souls who strive to put "Service Above Self" and to make the world a better place where "happily ever afters" are not merely the stuff of which fairy tales are made. I like to think that Hans Christian Andersen would want to join us for lunch!

BECAUSE OF ROTARY . . . I am currently writing a history book about Ballston Spa which includes an extensive chapter about that village's Rotary Club. As my way of returning the priceless gift that was given to me by Rotary International in 1971, a portion of the proceeds will be donated to support literacy programs at home and in the global community.

To learn more, please visit

www.ballstonsparotary.org

Ballston Spa

The Way We Were;

The Way We Are

Founded in 1807, Ballston Spa contains a treasure trove of fascinating and inspiring human interest stories waiting to be shared with contemporary readers and those of future generations.

What better time than the 200th anniversary of the upstate New York village's founding to publish a keepsake book that celebrates and commemorates the individuals and institutions that contributed to the enrichment and growth of the community over the past two centuries?

Ballston Spa: The Way We Were; The Way We Are will be a tribute to lives and legacies with well-researched tales of battles fought and lessons taught; of promises made and foundations laid; of good sports of all sorts; of mice that roared and visions restored; of dreams fulfilled . . . and as yet unfolding.

This limited edition book by Ann Hauprich will bring history to life in a way that instills pride in the village's past and present . . . and hope for many bright tomorrows.

To learn more, please visit www.annhauprich.com

146

Table of Contents

(A Sneak Peek)

Illustrated with contemporary photographs by Michael L. Noonan as well as images supplied by museums and private collectors, the keepsake-quality publication will feature chapters covering a broad spectrum of subjects. Chapters include (but are not limited to) the following:

Gone ... but worth remembering
Theaters, horse-drawn carriages, trains, trolleys, telegraphs, party lines, soda fountains, fashions & fads galore.

Hard acts to follow
Find out what went on behind-the-scenes during the shooting of some memorable scenes between actors Robert Redford & Barbra Steisand in "The Way We Were.

Houses of Worship
Heaven knows they've been an answer to a prayer in good times and bad!

Landmarks & Legends
Fascinating tales from Brookside, The Old Chocolate Factory, The Medbery & more!

Law & Order
Highlights of famous (and, in some cases, infamous) trials as well as tributes to some remarkable police officers and legal eagles.

Lest We Forget
Stories of sacrifice and heroism on the homefront during times of conflict and crisis . . . before, during and after 9/11.

Mayors & Milestones
More than meets the eye: Here's why!

Of pills, drills & assorted ills!
Docs who made house calls and dentists who made lasting impressions; life during pre-penicillin epidemics through to the amazing age of nuclear medicine.

Ruralities
From small family farms to gigantic agritourism destinations; the growth of Cornell Cooperative Extension & more!

School Days
A look back at one-room schoolhouses and how the village's education system has kept pace with the changing times.

Recreation & Leisure
What folks did for fun before television & computers . . . and why some forms of amusement never change!

Three Cheers for Volunteers!
In giving, they enriched (and sometimes saved) lives! From volunteer firefighters and service clubs to The Red Cross, The Center for HOPE . . . and legions more!

Tycoons & Dynasties
Entrepreneurs & innovators; movers & shakers . . . there's good reason why some businesses have been around for generations!

Do you need more
Laugh Lines?

This order form makes it easy
to share the joy with others!

Please send _____ copy/copies of

Deadlines, Headlines & Porcupines:
The Laugh Lines Behind the Bylines

to:

NAME: _____

ADDRESS: _____

_____

PRICE: $14.95 (US funds)

PLUS SHIPPING & HANDLING: $3.00 (US) for the first book;
$2.00 (US) additional book shipped to the same postal address.
Where applicable, please add $1.05 for New York State sales tax.

Kindly remit check or money order payable to:
ANN HAUPRICH COMMUNICATIONS
PO Box 2782, Malta, NY 12020

TOTAL AMOUNT ENCLOSED: $_____

Internet orders also accepted at: www.annhauprich.com